ON TARGET Special

CW00675917

Wings of Silver
The Silver Years of the RAF 1919–1939
By Mike Starmer and Peter Freeman

Introduction

This profile is a celebration of the Royal Air Force between the two World Wars. It was a short but intense period of development both in terms of technology and organisation. It was the proving ground for some of the most legendary aircraft of the Twentieth Century. It was also one of the most colourful and romantic periods of British aviation history. Silver-painted biplanes captivated audiences throughout the British Isles with their daring aerobatics, while others resolutely protected the far outposts of the British Empire. The spirit of the RAF is encapsulated within this era.

Peter Freeman

First published in Great Britain in 2007 by
The Aviation Workshop Publications Ltd
and Gary Madgwick
13 Charlton Road, Wantage, Oxon, OX12 8EP, UK
Tel: 01235 769038   Fax: 01235 771432
Email: aviation-workshop@btconnect.com
Website: www.theaviationworkshop.co.uk
Second edition 2008

Managing Editor Gary Madgwick
Front cover illustration and Project Management Andy Donovan
Book Editor Mike Shackleton AMR Design Ltd

Layout and design by
AMR Design Ltd.
Kestrel Court, Vyne Road, Sherborne St John,
Basingstoke, Hants, RG24 9HJ
Tel: 01256 889455   Fax: 01256 889430
www.amrdesign.com

Printed in England by PHP Litho Printers Ltd.
Hoyle Mill, Barnsley, South Yorkshire, S71 1HN

ISBN 1-904643-34-5

Distribution and marketing in the UK by The Aviation Workshop Publications Ltd.
Trade terms available on request.

The Globe is a registered trademark to The Aviation Workshop Publications Ltd.

All enquires regarding this publication, past publications or future projects and publications should be directed to the publishers.

Publisher's Note

In preparing this book, we have always tried to work from colour photographs and to confirm markings and serials from more than one source. In the few instances where photographs have not been available, great care has been taken to cross-reference all available data and research material. To this end the following books need mention:

Aircraft Camouflage and Markings 1907–1954, Bruce Robertson, Harleyford Publications Limited, 1956; *An Illustrated History of the RAF*, Roy Conyers Nesbit, Salamander Books Limited, 1994; *Bristol F.2B Fighter*, Chaz Bowyer, Ian Allan Ltd, 1985; *Bulldog – the Bristol Bulldog Fighter*, David Luff, Airlife Publications Ltd, 1987; *Eyes of the RAF – A History of Photo-Reconnaissance*, Roy Conyers Nesbit, Bramley Books, 1996; *Flying Units of the RAF*, Alan Lake, Airlife Publishing Ltd, 1999; *Gloster Gladiator*, Tom Spencer, Warpaint Series No.37, Warpaint Books Ltd; *Hawker Hurricane – RAF Northern Europe 1936–1945*, Camouflage and Markings, Ducimus Books Ltd; *On Silver Wings*, Alec Lumsden and Owen Thetford, Osprey Aerospace, 1993; *Pictorial History of the RAF. Vol.1 1918–1939*, J.W.R. Taylor and P.J.R. Moyes, Ian Allan 1968; *RAF Operations 1918–1938*, Chaz Bowyer, William Kimber & Co Ltd, 1988; *RAF Operations 1918–1938*, Chaz Bowyer, William Kimber & Co Ltd, 1988; *RAF Pilots in Training*, Major Oliver Stewart, MC AFC, War in the Air, Part 13, The Amalgamated Press Ltd, 1936; *Royal Air Force Fighters 1920–1929*, John D.R. Rawlings, Aerospace Publishing Ltd, 1996; *Royal Air Force Fighters 1919–1929*, John D.R. Rawlings, Wings of Fame Vol.5, Aerospace Publishing Ltd, 1996; *Royal Air Force Fighters 1930–1939*, Jon Lake, Wings of Fame Vol.16, Aerospace Publishing Ltd, 1999; *Royal Air Force Squadrons Partwork*, Orbis Publications, 1980, *Second to None, Shiny Two, 2 (AC) Squadron*, RAF, John Heathcott, Wings of Fame Vol.11, Aerospace Publishing Ltd, 1998; *Spitfire – A Complete Fighting History*, Alfred Price, The Promotional Reprint Company Limited, 1991; *Spitfire: a Test Pilot's Story*, Jeffrey Quill, Air Data Publications, 1996; *The Spitfire Story*, Alfred Price, Arms and Armour Press; *The Hart Family: Hawker Hart and Derivatives*, Aeroguide Classics No.5, Linewrights Ltd. 1989; *The RAF in Camera 1903–1939* by Roy Conyers Nesbit, Alan Sutton Publishing Limited in association with The Public Record Office, 1995; www.211squadron.org by D.R. Clark and others, 1998–2006; www.raf.mod.uk/downloads/gallery/h2238.jpg; www.rafmuseum.org 'Milestones of Flight'; www.shuttleworth.org; Private collection of John Adams; Private collection of Mike Starmer and various features from Aeroplane Magazine, Aircraft in Profile, Aeroplane Monthly, Aircraft Illustrated Extra, Aircraft Illustrated mnagazine, Aircraft Modelworld, Aviation News, Scale Aircraft Modelling, Scale Aviation Modeller International.

A very special thanks to Jon Freeman, Andy Donovan, Dale Clark, Benita Hiley, Mike Starmer, Tim Walsh, Brian House and the guys at Sheffield Model Club.

Dedication
To my father, Ian Madgwick. Thank you for building me those little Airfix biplanes that I had hung from my ceiling. They got me started on my life-long interest in aviation and modelling.

Gary Madgwick – March 2007

THE AVIATION WORKSHOP PUBLICATIONS LTD

Wings of Silver

The Silver Years of the RAF 1919–1939

Foreword

I am privileged to have been asked to write a foreword and short notes to this profile about the Royal Air Force entitled *Wings of Silver* which has been cleverly crafted by my associate Peter Freeman. The profiles here are original work created from photographs culled by myself and several other people from numerous published sources over many years. I have always been interested in aviation and in particular the colours and markings applied to the worlds air forces. As a result, I collected published material over most of my life with the view that at some time I, or someone else, might find this information useful. During production of this book, I was approached to give an opinion regarding the colours and markings of many of the machines shown in this book. Bearing in mind the pitfalls associated with assessing colour from monochrome photographs. I have done so to the best of my ability with the proviso that if there are errors, then the greater majority are mine.

At the time of the Armistice in 1918, air forces were still comparative newcomers to military affairs but by then the RAF had become the most powerful air force in the world. Stringent post-war economies coupled with a nationwide war-weary outlook obliged the government of the day to severely cut back on all military expenditure – in fact the RAF was almost entirely disbanded. A powerful and far-sighted lobby persisted and so the RAF remained but only as a mere shadow of its former self. Most squadrons were disbanded, reduced from 118 to only 12 by the end of 1919. Those that did remain were obliged to continue using the machines that they were equipped with when the war ended. In the fighter squadrons, common sense dictated that only the most up-to-date aircraft stayed in service so Sopwith Snipes and one squadron of Dolphin machines were kept whilst all of the older SE5 and Camel aircraft were sold or scrapped. However, by March 1920, such short-sightedness was perceived to be in error. By then there were twenty-five squadrons and by October 1924 had risen to forty-three. Severe financial economies prevailed until the 1930s when the expansion schemes began to take effect due to political events in Europe. These financial restrictions meant that technical development remained slow and dogma against monoplanes meant that the biplane layout with two-gun armament persisted until the mid-1930s when designers were at last able to show what they were capable of as more money became available. Within five years, features such as retractable undercarriages, enclosed cockpits and multi-gun armament that had been introduced gradually on foreign-designed aircraft now appeared almost simultaneously on newer British designs.

These profiles not only demonstrate the gradually changing aircraft themselves but the colours and finishes applied to them. Initially, machines carried their wartime finish, PC10 or PC12 dull Khaki on upper surfaces, with plain doped fabric underneath. Very shortly during refurbishment, a superior anti-UV light finish prevailed with the application of aluminium (Silver) based doped fabric with dull Silver anodised and later, polished natural metal panelling with occasionally Black or Battleship Grey cowlings as on Bristol F.2B machines. This basic finish remained generally unchanged until early 1938. In July 1936, the Air Ministry stipulated that trainer aircraft should be Yellow overall with natural metal cowlings, these being buffed to a high shine. Matters remained until the threat of yet another war during the Munich Crisis of August to September 1938 brought about the introduction of a two-coloured matt camouflage finish for upper surfaces, although initially the Silver underside remained as late as 1940 on some specific types of aircraft. Silver eventually gave way to under-surfaces of Black for bombers, which were intended to operate at night, and Black/White as a Fighter, Army Co-operation and Coastal Artillery Co-operation Commands friendly aircraft identification scheme. The Yellow on trainers was retained. This was necessary as the rudimentary Radio Direction Finding (later radar) equipment only looked out to sea and furthermore, since aircraft recognition as a skill was not a service requirement, plotting of overland machines was the duty of the Observer Corps and carried out purely by eye and sound. Although most members of this corps could accurately identify particular aircraft types, this was not then an official requirement, it only being necessary to report aircraft as bomber or fighter or other types.

National markings changed only gradually. The large Red/White/Blue roundels dating from 1918 on both wing surfaces were kept as were fuselage roundels and rudder stripes with Blue leading, all in bright shades. Under-wing serials had been applied to all training aeroplanes, mostly Avro 504K and N types from October 1918. Human spirit prevailed and more colour slowly crept onto the scene primarily to identify individual flights within a squadron as an aid to formation flying. By 18 December 1924, flight colours were officially allowed on wheel discs – 'A' flight to have red, 'B' flight to have Blue and 'C' flight

Yellow. However, no other components of the airframe were to be coloured. Shortly thereafter, a marking to identify particular squadrons began to creep in, usually applied to the fin. This could take the form of a single emblem or colours or an adaptation of the official squadron badge. Unofficially, flight colours had expanded to include spinners and in some cases fins, too. By 1924, the first span-wise, squadron-identifying coloured bars could be seen between the roundels on the upper-wing surfaces, a practice rapidly followed by other units until by 1930 it had become common, as were fuselage flashes in similar style. Whilst officialdom had perhaps encouraged this *esprit de corps* it had, however, taken the precaution of introducing Black under-wing serial numbers in March 1927, evidently to discourage the practice of low-flying and show-off manoeuvres. A further markings change came in September 1930 when the rudder striping was reversed from the earlier practice, now with Red leading against the rudder post. This lasted but a short time since in 1934, following fears of control surfaces over-balance due to weight of dope. The rudder stripes were discontinued and wing roundels were no longer allowed to impinge onto aileron surfaces. Only Black serial numbers were to be painted onto rudder surfaces, rear fuselage and under-wing. The Air Ministry officially started a practice which had begun in the 1930s by some squadrons with the use of a variation of the unit badge within an emblem. The new regulation required a formal sized outline frame with the unit crest set within it. The frames were a spear-head for fighters, a grenade for bombers and torpedo bombers and a six-pointed star for general reconnaissance and army co-operation squadrons. Although often applied in White or Silver, the background within the frame was sometimes coloured to accord with flight colours.

Since before 1936, the RAE at Farnborough had already been conducting camouflage trials for use on aircraft. During that year, one of the first types to have a trial scheme applied were some Avro Rota autogyro machines painted in Dark Earth, Dark Green, Light Earth and Light Green. The general introduction of camouflage by early 1938 brought a dull appearance to service machines. The new expansion types were factory finished in upper-surface disruptive camouflage, whilst those in service had it applied either at a maintenance unit (MU) or at squadron level. All bright squadron identification markings disappeared under coats of Dark Green and Dark Earth paint, some to the specified pattern whilst others simply carried alternate stripes of those colours. In some squadrons, the service badge was retained and usually units applied their new unit lettered identity codes in Medium Sea Grey or a similar mixture, in some cases before camouflage had been applied. While under-surfaces were supposed to have been equally divided into Black and White, this was very often only partially done, often in haste and unknowing of the intent due to ambiguous orders. Fear of overbalancing meant that Silver control surfaces often remained, as did whole tail surfaces. In some cases only Black was applied to the specified portions of the under-surfaces, the rest remaining Silver. There were numerous anomalies.

National marking roundels should have been repainted in newly devised dull shades with the White portion over-painted. However, both bright and dull colours and roundel styles could be seen on aeroplanes well into 1940. During this period a deal of variation and confusion remained. Eventually, the authorities came to grips with the problem and more formal and unambiguous orders came into play that helped to a great degree.

Having set the scene, I invite the reader to examine the profiles and imagine these in three-dimensional form in what was a golden age for the RAF. Not until 1946 did 'Silver' reappear and then only for a short period before giving way to camouflage once more during the Cold War and subsequent periods. However, colourful squadron markings did persist somewhat longer in some cases, albeit muted and reduced in size as they do to the present day.

Michael Starmer   2007

Sopwith 7F.1 Snipe, E8358, 'BONZO', RAF Pageant, Hendon, 30 June 1923. Pilot: Flight Lieutenant C.A. Stevens.

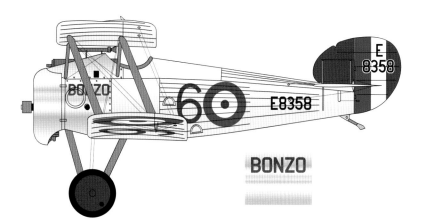

Air Displays and Air Races were a popular annual feature of the RAF during the 1920s and 30s. 'BONZO' was one of a three-aircraft team entered by the RAF School of Technical Training for Apprentices, Halton. Each team entered a Snipe, Brisfit and Avro for the Duke of York's Cup. This particular year, the Halton team won the cup. The large Red racing numbers on fuselage and wings would have been temporary markings. However, E8358 also carried flight recognition colours on its fin and wheel covers. Roundels were 25 inches in diameter on the fuselage and 56 inches in diameter on the upper- and lower-wing surfaces. The serials on both fuselage and rudder were 8 inches high and painted in Black (outlined in White on rudder).
Reference: p.17, *On Silver Wings*, Alec Lumsden and Owen Thetford, Osprey Aerospace, 1993.

Sopwith 7F.1 Snipe, E7538, 19 Squadron, Duxford, December 1924. Pilot: Flight Lieutenant West.

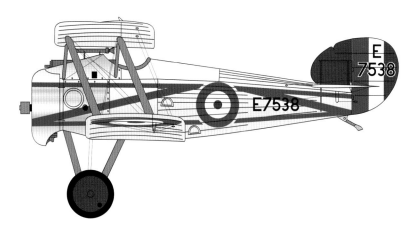

19 Squadron's first markings of the inter-war period were those carried by E7538. The Blue 'Z' and reverse 'Z' sit either side of the fuselage roundel. When replaced with the Gloster Grebe, these aircraft also, for a short while, carried the same marking. However, by mid-1926, 19 Squadron had adopted the familiar Blue and White chequer markings. Unfortunately, the Snipes would not have carried the chequer board markings as they had been phased out of service during 1926. Roundels were 25 inches in diameter on the fuselage and 56 inches in diameter on wing surfaces. Serials were 8 inches high on rudder and fuselage and painted in Black (outlined in White on rudder).
Reference: p.64, *A Question of Plumage*, Maurice Brett, Aeroplane Monthly, September 1994.

Sopwith 7F.1 Snipe, E6544, 17 Squadron, Hawkinge, 1924.

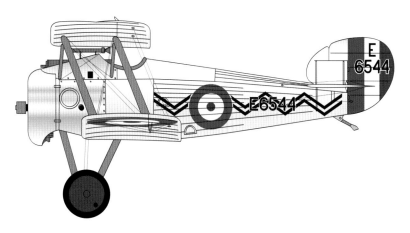

The well-known parallel Black zigzag marking of 17 Squadron was first introduced on the Snipe. This early version of the marking was over-painted with the fuselage serial number. E6544 also carried Red flight identification colours on its fin and wheel covers. Roundels were 25 inches in diameter on the fuselage and 56 inches in diameter on wing surfaces. Serials were painted in Black (outlined in White on the rudder) and 8 inches high on fuselage and rudder.
Reference: p.147, *Royal Air Force Fighters 1920–1929*, John D.R. Rawlings, Wings of Fame Vol.5, Aerospace Publishing Ltd. 1996.

Sopwith 7F.1 Snipe, F2441, 111 Squadron, Duxford, 1924.

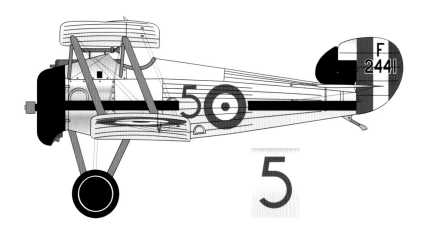

F2441 was another Air Race contestant and had a temporary racing number '5' added in Red. Air Races were extremely popular throughout the 1920s and the RAF used these events to both show off their latest equipment and also provide valuable experience for their pilots. The squadron marking of a Black band ran down the centre of the fuselage. Cowling, fin and wheel covers were also painted in Black. Unfortunately, no photographic reference has been found to ascertain whether the squadron markings were repeated on the upper-wing surfaces of Snipes during this period. Roundels were 25 inches in diameter on the fuselage and 56 inches in diameter on wing surfaces. The rudder serials were 8 inches high in Black with a White outline.
Reference: p.147, *Royal Air Force Fighters 1920–1929*, John D.R. Rawlings, Wings of Fame Vol.5, Aerospace Publishing Ltd. 1996.

Not to any scale

Sopwith 7F.1 Snipe, E6268, 32 Squadron, Kenley, 1924.

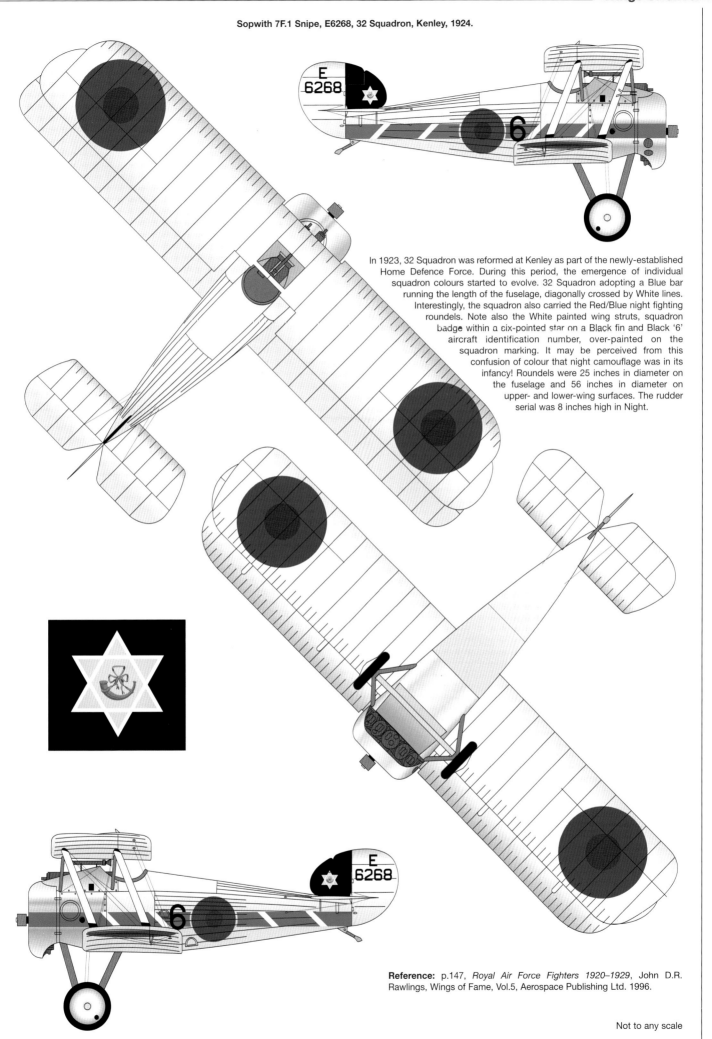

In 1923, 32 Squadron was reformed at Kenley as part of the newly-established Home Defence Force. During this period, the emergence of individual squadron colours started to evolve. 32 Squadron adopting a Blue bar running the length of the fuselage, diagonally crossed by White lines. Interestingly, the squadron also carried the Red/Blue night fighting roundels. Note also the White painted wing struts, squadron badge within a six-pointed star on a Black fin and Black '6' aircraft identification number, over-painted on the squadron marking. It may be perceived from this confusion of colour that night camouflage was in its infancy! Roundels were 25 inches in diameter on the fuselage and 56 inches in diameter on upper- and lower-wing surfaces. The rudder serial was 8 inches high in Night.

Reference: p.147, *Royal Air Force Fighters 1920–1929*, John D.R. Rawlings, Wings of Fame, Vol.5, Aerospace Publishing Ltd. 1996.

Not to any scale

Bristol F.2B Mk.III, F.4717, 'C' Flight, 2 (AC) Squadron, Andover, 1924.

'C' Flight of 2(AC) Squadron was identified by the central Blue stripe bordered by the two Red stripes around the fuselage. Between 1920 and 1922, the squadron was based in Ireland as part of 11 (Irish) Group with a Flight each at Castlebar and Fermoy. Its main duties were supporting the army with

reconnaissance and liaison flights during the Irish Rebellion. Roundels were 25 inches in diameter on the fuselage and 62 inches in diameter on the wing surfaces. Serials were 8 inches high on the fuselage and 6 inches high on the rudder all painted in Night.
Reference: p.64, *Bristol F.2B Fighter*, Chaz Bowyer, Ian Allan Ltd. 1985.

Bristol F.2B Mk.III, J.6648, 14 Squadon, Jerusalem, Palestine, May 1924.

14 Squadron had served in the Middle East during the First World War and was to continue in this theatre of operations continuously throughout the inter-war years. Its main role was to assist ground forces in quelling tribal disturbances, particularly in close liaison with RAF armoured car sections. By 1924, the squadron's F.2Bs had been strengthened by DH.9As whose greater range

extended the patrol area. J6648 carried the 'Ace of Spades' insignia on its fin, which probably was used as a flight identification symbol. Roundels were applied 25 inches in diameter on the fuselage and 62 inches on the wing surfaces. Serials were in Night and 8 inches high on the fuselage and 6 inches in height on the rudder.
Reference: p.5, *Bristol F.2B Fighter*, Chaz Bowyer, Ian Allan Ltd. 1985.

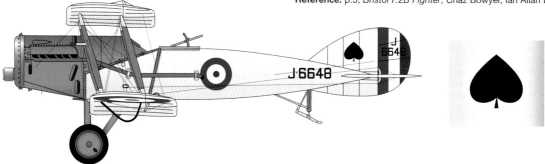

Bristol F.2B Mk.III, F.4500, 2 (AC) Squadron, Andover, 1925.

By the mid-1920s, 2 (AC) Squadron's three stripe fuselage markings were replaced with a Black triangle on the fin with a White 2. The origin of the triangle dates back to 1916 when 2 Squadron used it on their B.E.2 reconnaissance aircraft operating over the Somme. In 1927, 2 (AC) Squadron was again briefly posted overseas to China as a show of strength against Chinese Nationalists threatening British interests in that region. Based at Shanghai Racecourse, the

squadron flew reconnaissance and liaison sorties. Roundels were 25 inches in diameter on the fuselage and 62 inches in diameter on the wing surfaces. Serials were 8 inches high on the fuselage and 6 inches high on the rudder all painted in Night.
Reference: p.145, *Second to None, Shiny Two, No. II (AC) Squadron, RAF*, John Heathcott, Wings of Fame Vol. 11, Aerospace Publishing Ltd. 1998.

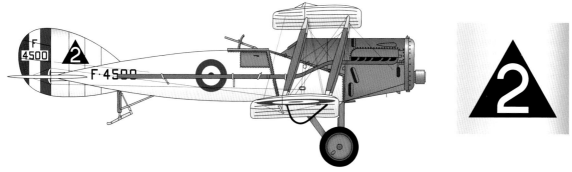

Bristol F.2B Mk.III, J8430, Royal Flight, Mousehole Heath Airport, Norwich, 1928.

J8430 was converted for the specific use of HRH Edward, Prince of Wales (later to be HM King Edward VIII). The Prince of Wales was a keen flyer, making his first flight in 1917 when he was a Major in the Grenadier Guards. Note the specially designed rear seat windshield and the Red chevron on the fin, which became the initial insignia for the Royal Flight. J8430 carried the larger fuselage

roundel of 30 inches in diameter, while the wing roundels were 62 inches in diameter. Serials were in Night and 8 inches high on the fuselage and 6 inches high on the rudder. Under-wing serials were 30 inches in height and also in Night.
Reference: p.71, *Bristol F.2B Fighter*, Chaz Bowyer, Ian Allan Ltd. 1985.

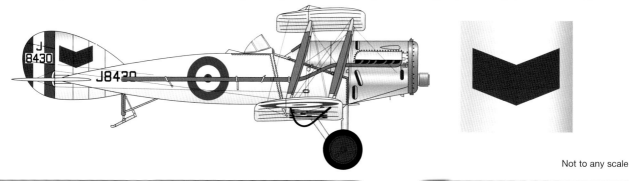

Not to any scale

Bristol F.2B Mk.III, J6662, 'B' Flight, 2 (AC) Squadron, Andover, 1924.

Prior to this period, 2 (AC) Squadron had spent ten years at Oranmore in Ireland supporting the army against the Sinn Fein rebellion. In recognition of its army co-operation role, the squadron was granted the distinguishing title of AC (Army Co-operation). 2 (AC) Squadron flew F.2Bs when first formed in 1920 through to December 1929 when they were replaced with the Armstrong Whitworth Atlas. The squadron markings consisted of two Red fuselage bands separated by the flight colour. These were White for 'A' Flight, Yellow for 'B' Flight and Blue for 'C' Flight. Fuselage roundels were 25 inches in diameter and wing roundels 62 inches in diameter. Serials were in Night (outlined in White on rudder) and were 8 inches high on the fuselage and 6 inches high on rudder

Reference: p.145, *Second to None, Shiny Two, No. II (AC) Squadron, RAF,* John Heathcott, Wings of Fame Vol. 11, Aerospace Publishing Ltd. 1998.

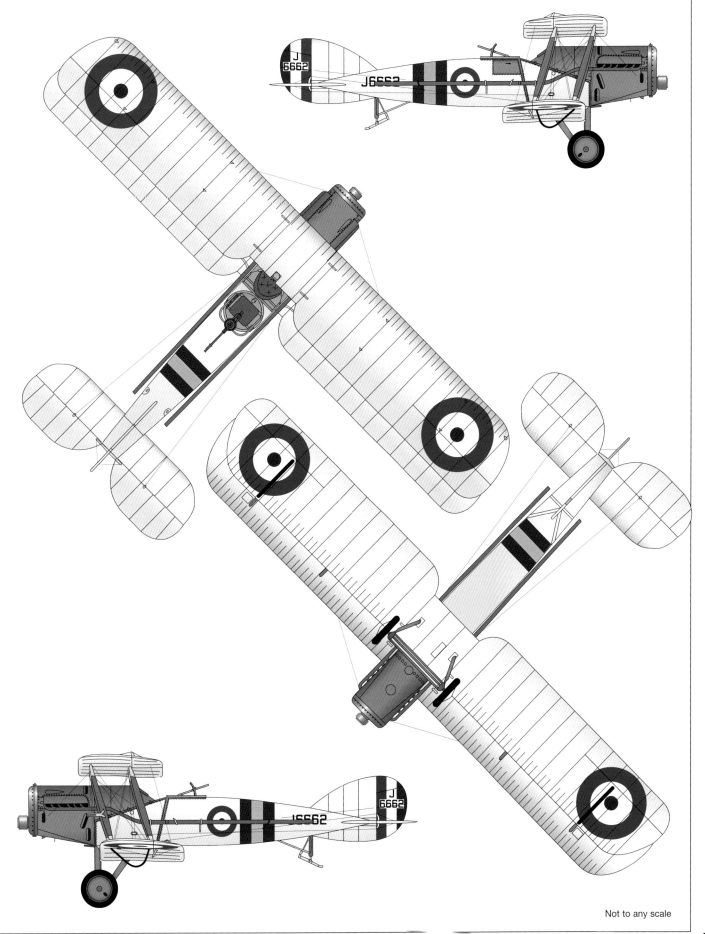

Not to any scale

Bristol F.2B Mk.II, H1492, 'A' Flight, 208 Squadron, Ismailia, Egypt, 1924.

208 Squadron adopted a colourful method of designating their flights using the suit symbols from playing cards. 'A' Flight were designated the 'Club' symbol, other flights selecting from the 'Heart, 'Diamond' and 'Spade' symbols. As well as displaying the club inside a White circle on the fin, the flight recognition symbol also appeared large on the under surface of the starboard lower-wing and centrally on the top wing. 208 Squadron spent many of its years of service on overseas deployment. Its main role was protecting British interests in the Suez Canal, but detachments also briefly saw action in the 'Chanak' crisis in Turkey as part of the RAF 'Constantinople Wing' and in Palestine. Roundels were 25 inches in diameter on the fuselage and 62 inches in diameter on wing surfaces. Serials were 8 inches high on the fuselage and 6 inches high on the rudder, both in Night, but with a White outline on the rudder serials.

Reference: p.86, *Bristol F.2B Fighter*, Chaz Bowyer, Ian Allan Ltd. 1985.

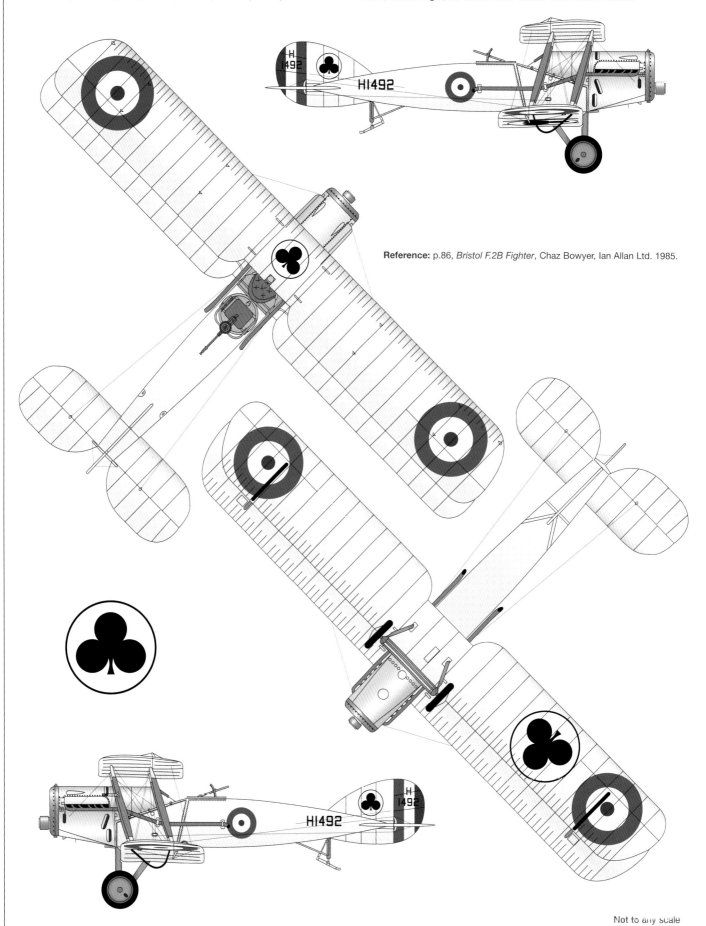

Not to any scale

Bristol F.2B Mk.IV, J8257, Oxford University Air Squadron, Abingdon, July 1928.

University Air Squadrons, initially Cambridge and Oxford, were established by Air Marshall Lord Trenchard in 1925. He believed that the RAF needed to attract a large proportion of intelligent and well-educated recruits into the service and saw university graduates as ideal candidates. The Air Squadrons were to act as an introduction to flying and many graduates were to later continue their training officially through Cranwell and other Flying Training Schools. The distinguishing 'Oxford Blue' band down the fuselage and top wing was the squadron marking. On the fuselage, over-painted in Red outlined in White, was the large individual aircraft identification letter.

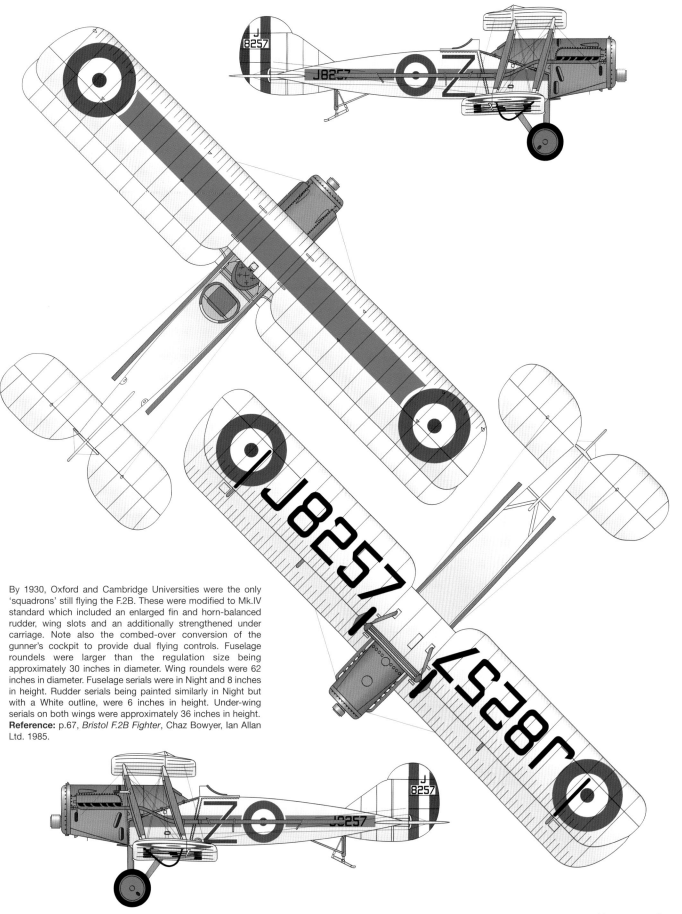

By 1930, Oxford and Cambridge Universities were the only 'squadrons' still flying the F.2B. These were modified to Mk.IV standard which included an enlarged fin and horn-balanced rudder, wing slots and an additionally strengthened under carriage. Note also the combed-over conversion of the gunner's cockpit to provide dual flying controls. Fuselage roundels were larger than the regulation size being approximately 30 inches in diameter. Wing roundels were 62 inches in diameter. Fuselage serials were in Night and 8 inches in height. Rudder serials being painted similarly in Night but with a White outline, were 6 inches in height. Under-wing serials on both wings were approximately 36 inches in height. **Reference**: p.67, *Bristol F.2B Fighter*, Chaz Bowyer, Ian Allan Ltd. 1985.

Not to any scale

Bristol F.2B Mk.II, FR4589, 208 Squadron, Heliopolis, Egypt 1927.

FR4589 belonged to the 'Ace of Hearts' flight of 208 Squadron – each flight was identified by one of the aces in a pack of cards. While being based in Egypt, detachments of the squadron were regularly sent to Palestine and Iraq, to support army operations against rebel tribes. The addition of the letter 'R' to the serial prefix denotes that this aircraft was a locally rebuilt machine carried out in-theatre. Roundels were 25 inches in diameter on the fuselage and 62 inches in diameter on the wing surfaces. Serials were in Night (with White outline on rudder) and were 8 inches in height on the fuselage and 6 inches in height on the rudder.

Reference: p.89, *Bristol F.2B Fighter*, Chaz Bowyer, Ian Allan Ltd. 1985.

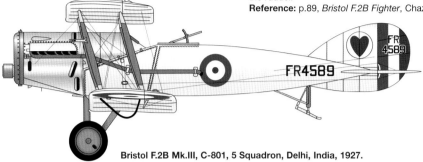

Bristol F.2B Mk.III, C-801, 5 Squadron, Delhi, India, 1927.

5 Squadron was one of the units which took part in operations against rebel tribesmen on the North-west Frontier of India. Of note was their distinguished service in what was named 'Pink's War' after the commander of air operations, Wing Commander R.C.M. Pink. The 'war' itself consisted of punitive raids against the Mahsud tribesmen of South Waziristan. Warning leaflets were often dropped prior to bombing raids, but 5 Squadron also undertook night bombing raids to harass the enemy around the clock. C-801 carried regulation roundels which were 25 inches in diameter on the fuselage and 62 inches in diameter on wing surfaces. Serials were in Night and were 8 inches high on the fuselage and 6 inches high on the rudder all in Night. The aircraft also carried a large letter 'A' as its identification number and also the squadron number on the fin.

Reference: p.19, *Pink's War – the Turning Point,* Chaz Bowyer, Aircraft Illustrated Extra No. 6, Ian Allan Ltd.

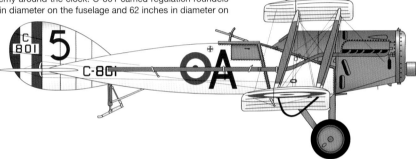

Bristol F.2B Mk.III, J6752, 20 Squadron, Peshawar, India, 1928.

20 Squadron saw active service in India from the end of the Great War right through to 1947. During the 1920s much of its time was spent on the North-west Frontier between India and Afghanistan. Here, regular patrols were required to keep the constantly feuding tribes of this region from attacking each other. The Kashmir and Hindu Kush mountainous landscape and the ferocious tribesmen made each patrol long and difficult. Many of 20 Squadron's aircraft had seen action in the 1914-18 war and were still carrying bullet hole patches in their fabric! J6752 carried the larger fuselage roundel of 30 inches in diameter while the wing surface roundels were 62 inches in diameter. The large 'K' on the fin was the aircraft identification letter and was quite possibly also displayed on the under surface of the lower wing. Serials were in Night and were 8 inches high on the fuselage and 6 inches high on the rudder.

Reference: p.64, *Bristol F.2B Fighter*, Chaz Bowyer, Ian Allan Ltd. 1985.

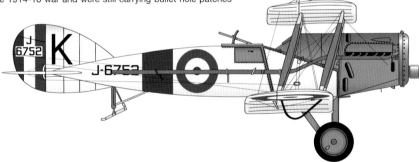

Bristol F.2B Mk.III, FR4744, 6 Squadron, Ismalia, Egypt, 1931.

6 Squadron finally relinquished their F.2Bs in 1931 when they were replaced with Fairey Gordons. Right up until their retirement, the F.2Bs of 6 Squadron were keeping the peace between Jew and Arab factions in Palestine and Iraq. The FR serial prefix denotes this aircraft as another refurbished machine, rebuilt locally. As an aircraft, which first saw action in 1917, it was a testimony to its flying qualities that it continued in front line service with the RAF for fourteen years. The squadron insignia of an eagle attacking a snake is displayed within a Red badge on the fin. Roundels were 30 inches in diameter on the fuselage and 62 inches in diameter on the wing surfaces. Serials were in Night (with White outline on rudder) and were 8 inches in height on the fuselage and 6 inches in height on the rudder.

Reference: p.90, *Bristol F.2B Fighter*, Chaz Bowyer, Ian Allan Ltd. 1985.

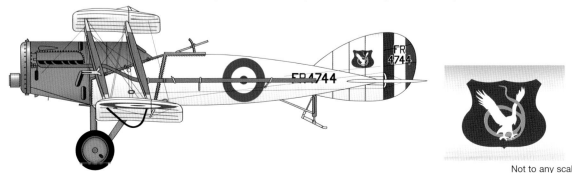

Not to any scale

De Havilland DH.9A, J.7124, 30 Squadron, Baghdad West, Iraq, August 1924. Pilot: Flight Lieutenant S.M. Kinkead.

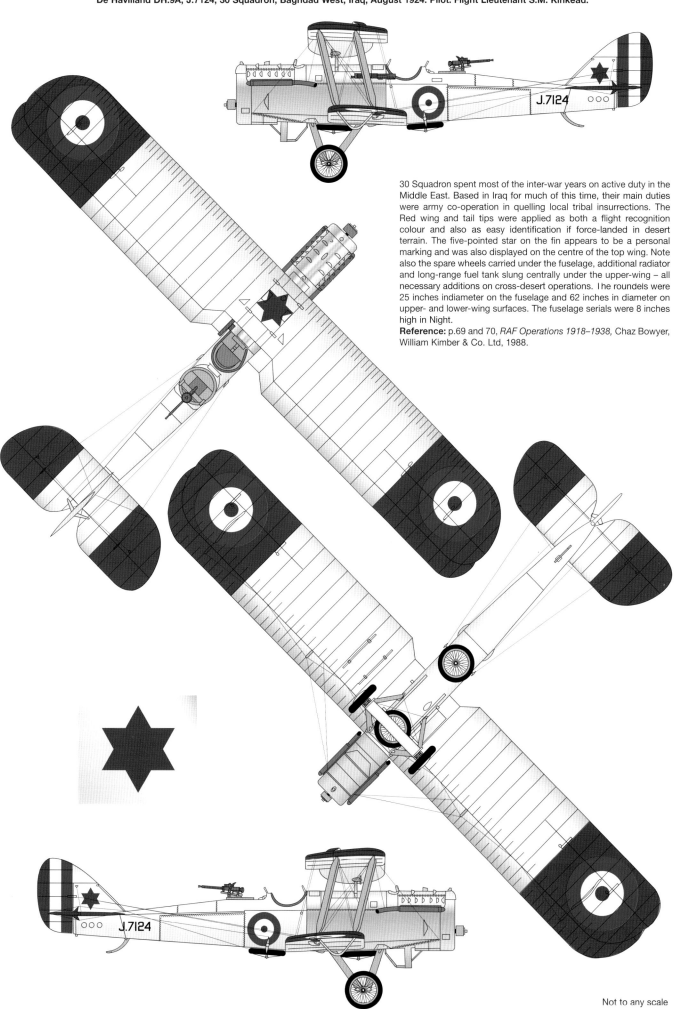

30 Squadron spent most of the inter-war years on active duty in the Middle East. Based in Iraq for much of this time, their main duties were army co-operation in quelling local tribal insurrections. The Red wing and tail tips were applied as both a flight recognition colour and also as easy identification if force-landed in desert terrain. The five-pointed star on the fin appears to be a personal marking and was also displayed on the centre of the top wing. Note also the spare wheels carried under the fuselage, additional radiator and long-range fuel tank slung centrally under the upper-wing – all necessary additions on cross-desert operations. The roundels were 25 inches indiameter on the fuselage and 62 inches in diameter on upper- and lower-wing surfaces. The fuselage serials were 8 inches high in Night.

Reference: p.69 and 70, *RAF Operations 1918–1938,* Chaz Bowyer, William Kimber & Co. Ltd, 1988.

Not to any scale

De Havilland DH.9A, E8650, 'A' Flight, 84 Squadron, Shaibah, Iraq, 1923. Pilot: Flying Officer F.F. Inglis.

84 Squadron established a tradition of using the four suites in a pack of playing cards for their flight recognition markings. They saw continual service in the Middle East throughout the 1920s, regularly supporting ground forces in their fight against Sheikh Mahmud's rebellious tribesmen. Note the alternative fixing place for the spare wheel and lack of wheel covers. Roundels were 28 inches in diameter on the fuselage and 62 inches in diameter on the upper- and lower-wing surfaces. Serials were painted in Night, outlined in White, being 8 inches high on the fuselage.
Reference: p.68, *RAF Operations 1918–1938*, Chaz Bowyer, William Kimber & Co. Ltd, 1988.

De Havilland DH.9A, E8723, 27 Squadron, Miramshah, India, 1925.

27 Squadron was another long-serving veteran of the RAF's involvement in the Far East. 1925 saw the continuation of tribal rebellion on the North-west Frontier with Afghanistan. This particular conflict became known as 'Pink's War', named after the commanding officer of No.2 (India) Wing, Wing Commander R.C.M. Pink, whose leadership quelled the uprising after a period of fifty-four days. More importantly, it was the first opportunity for the RAF to carry out completely independent operations without the support of other services. Although only minor in scale, it set a precedent for future RAF operations in the critical years to come. E8723 carried the traditional 'Green Elephant' squadron emblem on the fin and its individual aircraft number beneath the exhaust, signifying aircraft 'A' of 'A' Flight. Roundels were 28 inches in diameter on the fuselage and 62 inches on the upper- and lower-wing surfaces. Serials were in Night, (outlined in White on rudder), being 8 inches high on the fuselage and 6 inches on the rudder.

Reference: p.17, *Pink's War – The Turning Point,* Chaz Bowyer, Aircraft Illustrated Extra No.6, Ian Allan Ltd.

De Havilland DH.9A, H3510, 8 Squadron, Baghdad, Iraq, 1926.

8 Squadron was reformed in Egypt in 1921 and was moved that year to Baghdad to support the quelling of a tribal insurrection by Sheikh Mahmud, the self-styled 'King of Kurdistan'. The rebellion sporadically went on until 1931 when Mahmud finally surrendered to the RAF. H3510 carried the essential desert extras of spare wheel slung under the fuselage, long-range fuel tank under the top wing and additional radiator attached under the nose. The Red fin was possibly a flight recognition marking and the individual aircraft code on the fuselage was often repeated below either both or one of the lower under-wing surfaces. Roundels were 28 inches on the fuselage and 62 inches on the upper- and lower-wing surfaces. Serials were in Night, (outlined in White on rudder) being 8 inches high on the fuselage and rudder. The large individual aircraft identification letter was also in Night.

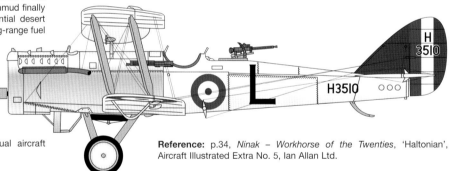

Reference: p.34, *Ninak – Workhorse of the Twenties,* 'Haltonian', Aircraft Illustrated Extra No. 5, Ian Allan Ltd.

De Havilland DH.9A, H-72, 27 Squadron, Risalpur, India, 1927.

Towards the end of 1926, much of the troubles on the North-west Frontier had been temporarily subdued. It was decided in early 1927 to hold a Grand Air Display, similar to those held at Hendon, at Delhi Racecourse. 27 Squadron was one of the units which took part, performing full squadron take-offs simultaneously with 60 Squadron. More regular duties for the squadron continued in their operational theatre with 'demonstration' flights over troublesome tribal villages, protection of army relief columns to their outposts and the unending reconnaissance and aerial mapping. H-72 showed a change in squadron markings to a large number '27' on the fin and individual aircraft identification letter in a Black square on the fuselage. Roundels were 28 inches in diameter on the fuselage and 62 inches in diameter on the upper- and lower-wing surfaces. Serials were in Night, being 8 inches high on the fuselage and rudder. Note the extra large White box for the rudder serial rather than the usual White outline.

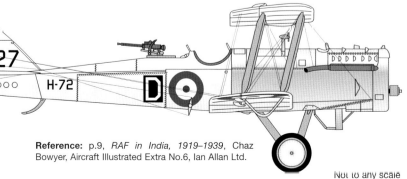

Reference: p.9, *RAF in India, 1919–1939*, Chaz Bowyer, Aircraft Illustrated Extra No.6, Ian Allan Ltd.

Not to any scale

De Havilland DH.9A, J.7086, 'B' Flight, 47 Squadron, Helwan, Egypt, 1928. Pilot: Flight Lieutenant S.D. MacDonald.

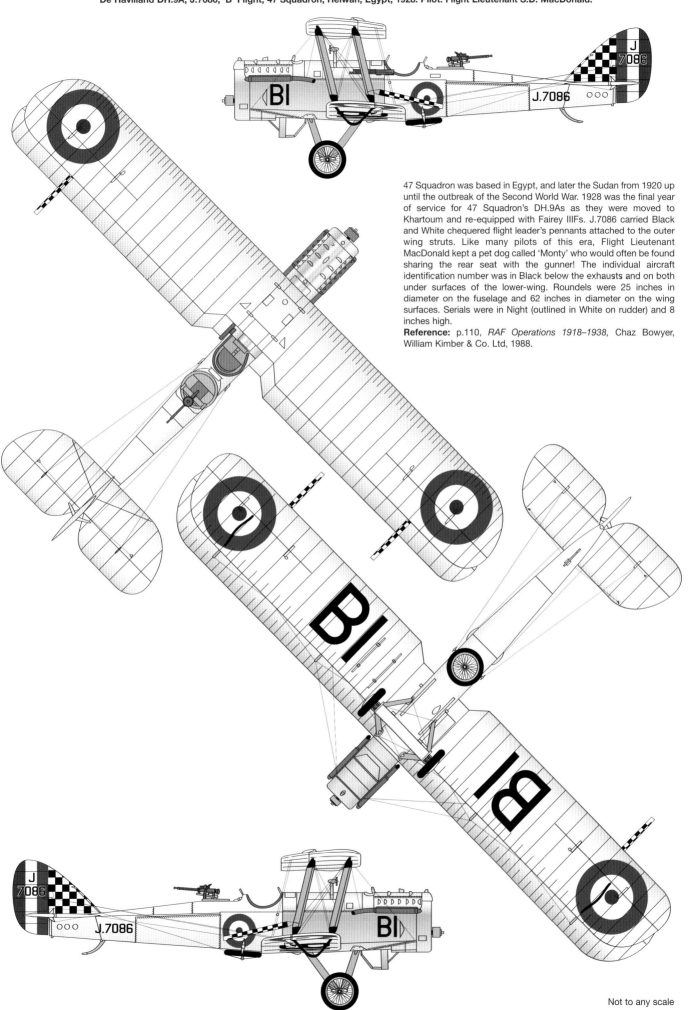

47 Squadron was based in Egypt, and later the Sudan from 1920 up until the outbreak of the Second World War. 1928 was the final year of service for 47 Squadron's DH.9As as they were moved to Khartoum and re-equipped with Fairey IIIFs. J.7086 carried Black and White chequered flight leader's pennants attached to the outer wing struts. Like many pilots of this era, Flight Lieutenant MacDonald kept a pet dog called 'Monty' who would often be found sharing the rear seat with the gunner! The individual aircraft identification number was in Black below the exhausts and on both under surfaces of the lower-wing. Roundels were 25 inches in diameter on the fuselage and 62 inches in diameter on the wing surfaces. Serials were in Night (outlined in White on rudder) and 8 inches high.

Reference: p.110, *RAF Operations 1918–1938,* Chaz Bowyer, William Kimber & Co. Ltd, 1988.

Not to any scale

De Havilland DH.9A, H3632, 30 Squadron, Baghdad West, Iraq, August 1924.

During 1924, 30 Squadron was kept busy quelling the rebellious tribesmen that followed Sheikh Mahmud in and around Kirkuk. In the north, they were also helping prohibit Turkish advances into Mosul. H3632 carried an individual aircraft identification symbol in the form of a swastika. For a while, the squadron used this form of marking rather than letters or numbers to identify its aircraft. Note also the Red tips to main and tail planes serving a dual purpose of flight identification and as a rescue aid if a desert forced-landing was necessary. Roundels were 28 inches on the fuselage and 62 inches on the upper- and lower-wing surfaces. Serials were in Night (outlined in White on rudder) being 8 inches high on both the fuselage and rudder.
Reference: p.70, *RAF Operations 1918–1938*, Chaz Bowyer, William Kimber & Co. Ltd, 1988.

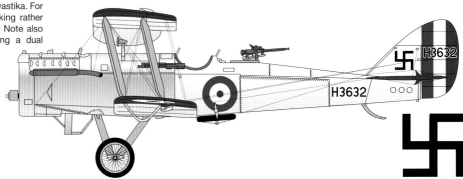

De Havilland DH.9A, J7256, 'C' Flight, 55 Squadron, Hinaidi, Iraq, 1926.

55 Squadron spent much of 1926 assisting ground troops in quelling Sheikh Mahmud's rebel tribesmen as they tried to infiltrate friendly villages in the Kirkuk region. J7256 carried the distinctive Black chequer band around the fuselage and radiator. Note also the Roman numerals used for aircraft identification. Roundels were 28 inches on the fuselage and 62 inches on the upper- and lower-wing surfaces. Serials were in Night, (outlined in White on rudder) being 8 inches high on the fuselage and rudder.
Reference: p.73, *RAF Operations 1918–1938,* Chaz Bowyer, William Kimber & Co. Ltd, 1988.

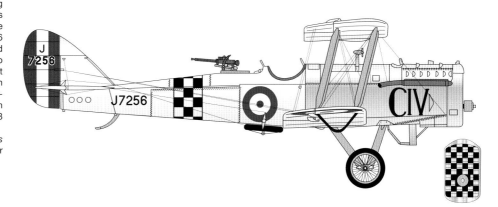

De Havilland DH.9A, J.8184, 600 (City of London) Squadron, Royal Auxiliary Air Force, Northolt, 1926.

600 Squadron was formed at Northolt on 14 October 1925 as a unit of the Auxiliary Air Force. Equipped with DH.9As and Avro 504Ns, it operated as a day bomber squadron until 1934. J.8184 carried the City of London crest beneath the exhaust, the squadron number on the rear fuselage and aircraft identification number below and forward of the cockpit. Also of note is the addition of what appears to be a small glazed panel at the bottom of the gunner's compartment and a camera gun in the Scarff Ring. Roundels were 28 inches on the fuselage and 62 inches on the upper- and lower-wing surfaces. Serials were in Night (with White outline on rudder) being 8 inches high on both the fuselage and rudder.

Reference: p.21, *By Day and by Night*, Owen Thetford, Aeroplane Monthly, August 1992.

De Havilland DH.9A, E944, 30 Squadron, Hinaidi, Iraq, 1928.

E944 carried the squadron insignia of a palm tree on a White disc on the fin. The aircraft identification letter 'X' appears on the fuselage and also on the under-wing surfaces and quite possibly on the centre section of the upper wing. The squadron's main area of operations around this period was in policing the feuding tribes on the Iraq-Kuwait border. Roundels were 28 inches on the fuselage and 62 inches on the upper- and lower-wing surfaces. Serials were in Night on a White background, being 8 inches high on the fuselage.
Reference: p.70, *RAF Operations 1918–1938,* Chaz Bowyer, William Kimber & Co. Ltd, 1988.

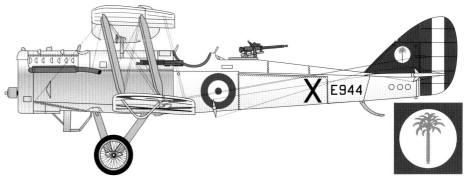

Not to any scale

Avro 504K, H2367, 'D' Flight, 4 Flying Training School, Abu Sueir, Egypt 1924.

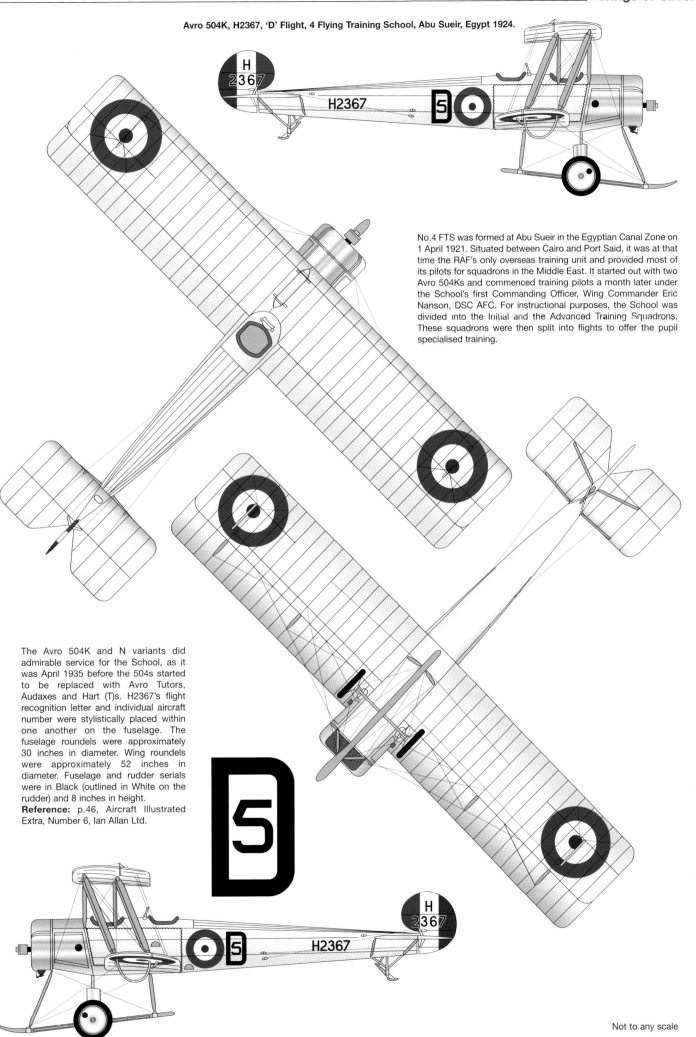

No.4 FTS was formed at Abu Sueir in the Egyptian Canal Zone on 1 April 1921. Situated between Cairo and Port Said, it was at that time the RAF's only overseas training unit and provided most of its pilots for squadrons in the Middle East. It started out with two Avro 504Ks and commenced training pilots a month later under the School's first Commanding Officer, Wing Commander Eric Nanson, DSC AFC. For instructional purposes, the School was divided into the Initial and the Advanced Training Squadrons. These squadrons were then split into flights to offer the pupil specialised training.

The Avro 504K and N variants did admirable service for the School, as it was April 1935 before the 504s started to be replaced with Avro Tutors, Audaxes and Hart (T)s. H2367's flight recognition letter and individual aircraft number were stylistically placed within one another on the fuselage. The fuselage roundels were approximately 30 inches in diameter. Wing roundels were approximately 52 inches in diameter. Fuselage and rudder serials were in Black (outlined in White on the rudder) and 8 inches in height.
Reference: p.46, Aircraft Illustrated Extra, Number 6, Ian Allan Ltd.

Not to any scale

Avro 504N, J.8504, 601 (County of London) Squadron, Northolt, Middlesex, October 1925.

601 Squadron was formed in 1925 as a light bomber squadron of the Auxiliary Air Force. Initially equipped with Avro 504Ns, these were replaced by DH9s in 1926, although the Avros continued in service as training aircraft. J.8504 displaysed its squadron insignia on the fuselage next to the squadron number in Red. The roundels were approximately 30 inches in diameter on the fuselage and 52 inches in diameter on wing surfaces. Serials were in Black (outlined in White on rudder) and were 8 inches high on fuselage and rudder. Under-wing serials appear to be approximately 30 inches in height and were also in Black.

Reference: p.108, *The RAF in Camera 1903–1939*, Roy Conyers Nesbit, Alan Sutton Publishing Limited in association with The Public Record Office, 1995.

Avro 504N, J.8527, Cambridge University Air Squadron, 1927.

Cambridge University formed the first ever University Air Squadron and started enrolling prospective pilots on 1st October 1925. All the members were undergraduates of the University, the very first member being G.H. Watkins, the famous explorer who pioneered expeditions on the Arctic air routes in Greenland. J.8527 carried the distinctive 'Cambridge Blue' Light Blue band outlined in darker Blue around the fuselage. The squadron badge incorporated the university coat of arms and appears beneath the front cockpit. The roundels were approximately 30 inches in diameter on the fuselage and 52 inches in diameter on wing surfaces. Serials were in Night (outlined in White on rudder) and were 8 inches high on fuselage and rudder. Under-wing serials appear to be approximately 30 inches in height and were also in Black.

Reference: p.64, *An Illustrated History of the RAF*, Roy Conyers Nesbit, Salamander Books Limited, 1994.

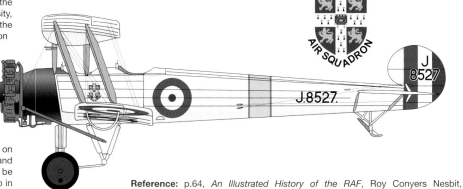

Avro 504N, J8978, 4 Flying Training School, Abu Sueir, Egypt, 1930.

4 Flying Training School was established at Abu Sueir in 1921 and continued to train pilots right up to the outbreak of the Second World War. The abundance of flat desert terrain and good flying weather made Abu Sueir an ideal training ground for novice pilots. J.8978 carried a Red sash and Black identification number on the fuselage. Roundels were 30 inches in diameter on fuselage and 52 inches in diameter on wing surfaces. Fuselage and rudder serials were in Black (with White outline on rudder) and were 8 inches high. Under-wing serials were also in Black and were approximately 30 inches in height.

Reference: p.105, *Flying Units of the RAF*, Alan Lake, Airlife Publishing Ltd. 1999.

Avro 504N, K.1812, Oxford University Air Squadron, Eastchurch Camp, 1934.

Oxford University Air Squadron was the second UAS to be formed – this took place on 11 October 1925 but it was January 1928 before flying commenced from Upper Heyford. It moved to Abingdon in November 1932 but closed on 3 September 1939. K.1812 carried the distinctive 'Oxford Blue' band along the fuselage and across the top wing. Note that the wheel covers were also painted in Blue. Over-painted in Black on the fuselage band was the individual aircraft identification letter and a small OUAS badge, bearing the Oxford University crest appears below the front cockpit. Roundels were approximately 30 inches in diameter on the fuselage and 52 inches in diameter on wing surfaces. Serials were in Black (outline in White on rudder) and 8 inches high on fuselage and rudder and approximately 30 inches high on the under surfaces of the lower wings.

Reference: From the artist's own photographic collection.

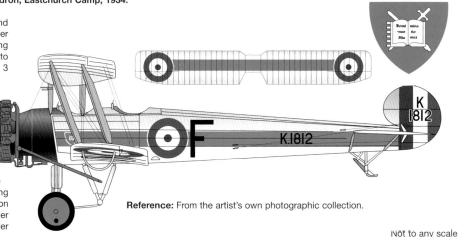

Not to any scale

Gloster Grebe Mk.II, J-7363, 25 Squadron, Hawkinge, mid-1926. Pilot: Squadron Leader Peck.

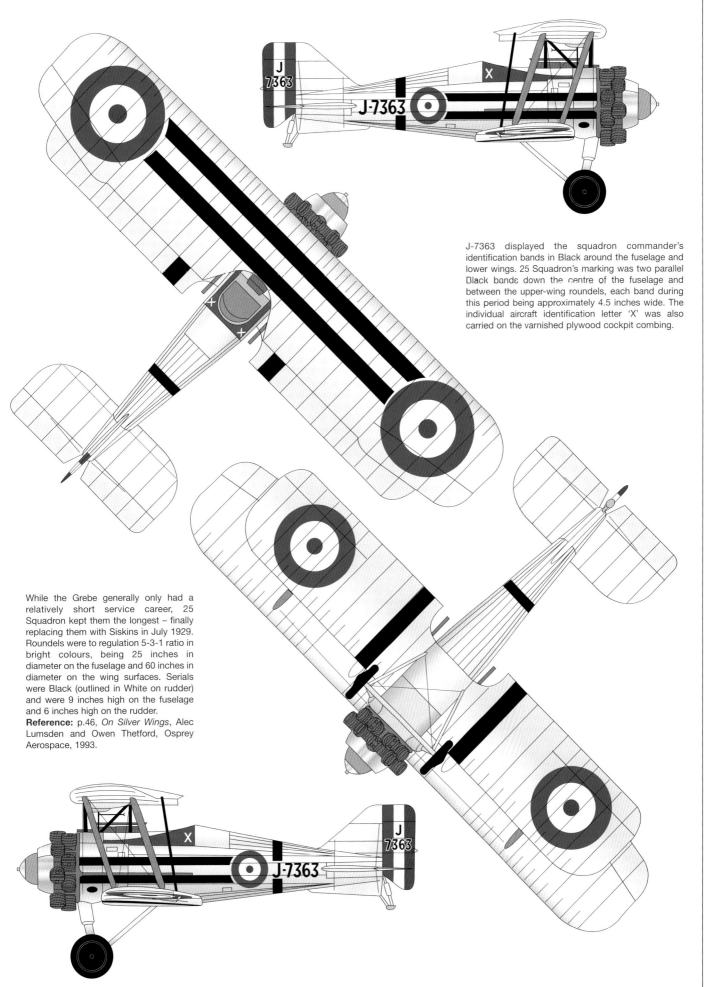

J-7363 displayed the squadron commander's identification bands in Black around the fuselage and lower wings. 25 Squadron's marking was two parallel Black bands down the centre of the fuselage and between the upper-wing roundels, each band during this period being approximately 4.5 inches wide. The individual aircraft identification letter 'X' was also carried on the varnished plywood cockpit combing.

While the Grebe generally only had a relatively short service career, 25 Squadron kept them the longest – finally replacing them with Siskins in July 1929. Roundels were to regulation 5-3-1 ratio in bright colours, being 25 inches in diameter on the fuselage and 60 inches in diameter on the wing surfaces. Serials were Black (outlined in White on rudder) and were 9 inches high on the fuselage and 6 inches high on the rudder.
Reference: p.46, *On Silver Wings*, Alec Lumsden and Owen Thetford, Osprey Aerospace, 1993.

Not to any scale

Gloster Grebe II, J-7413, 56 Squadron, Biggin Hill, 1924.

56 Squadron received their Grebes in September 1924. Their Red and White chequer marking was still seeing changes through this period. Quite often the number of chequers varied with the rank of the pilot. Some of 56 Squadron's aircraft still carried the tapering band of chequers, as the earlier style on the Snipe, although the parallel band was to become the standard for the design. The Squadron flew the Grebe for three years before transferring to Siskins. Roundels were to 25 inches in diameter on the fuselage and 60 inches in diameter on the wing surfaces. Serials were in Black (outlined in White on rudder) and were 9 inches high on the fuselage and 6 inches high on the rudder.

Reference: p.45, *On Silver Wings*, Alec Lumsden and Owen Thetford, Osprey Aerospace, 1993.

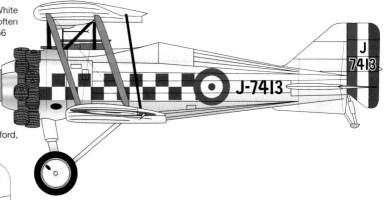

Gloster Grebe II, J-7588, 32 Squadron, Kenley, 1925.

32 Squadron's marking was a Blue band running down the centre of the fuselage and across the upper wing, with diagonal gaps at approximately 45 degrees. It was interesting to note that the earlier use of the White diagonal bars, as seen on their Sopwith Snipes, was left out leaving a much simpler design. Roundels were to 25 inches in diameter on the fuselage and 60 inches in diameter on the wing surfaces. Serials were in Black (outlined in White on rudder) and were 9 inches high on the fuselage and 6 inches high on the rudder.

Reference: p.41, *On Silver Wings*, Alec Lumsden and Owen Thetford, Osprey Aerospace, 1993.

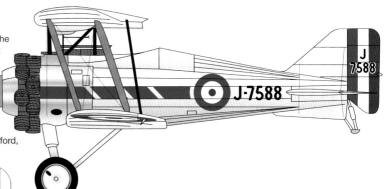

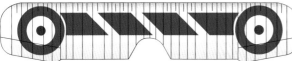

Gloster Grebe II, J-7390, 19 Squadron, Duxford, 1926.

J-7390 carried the early squadron marking of two thin parallel lines running centrally down the fuselage with two broader mirrored diagonals crossing them. By mid-1926, this was replaced by the well-known Blue and White chequered band down the fuselage and across the upper-wing. Roundels were to 25 inches in diameter on the fuselage and 60 inches in diameter on the wing surfaces. Serials were Black (outlined in White on rudder) and were 9 inches high on the fuselage and 6 inches high on the rudder.

Reference: p.64, *A Question of Plumage*, Maurice Brett, Aeroplane Monthly, September 1994.

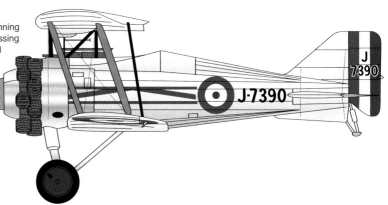

Gloster Grebe II, J7386, 19 Squadron, Duxford, 1927.

By the latter part of 1926, 19 Squadron had replaced their earlier markings with Blue and White chequers. Originally these were seven 9 inches squares along the fuselage. With early photographs it was sometimes difficult to differentiate between squadrons carrying chequer markings (e.g. 56 and 19 Squadrons). As a rough guide, 19 Squadron had fewer and bigger squares than its squadron rivals. Roundels were to 25 inches in diameter on the fuselage and 60 inches in diameter on the wing surfaces. Serials were in Black (outlined in White on rudder) and were 9 inches high on the fuselage and 6 inches high on the rudder.

Reference: p.151, *Royal Air Force Fighters 1920–1929*, John D.R. Rawlings, Wings of Fame, Vol.5, Aerospace Publishing Ltd. 1996.

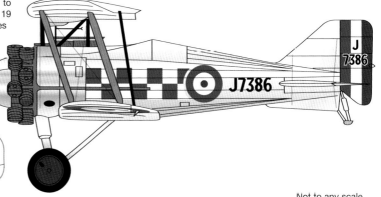

Not to any scale

Gloster Grebe Mk.II, J7593, 29 Squadron, Duxford, 1926.

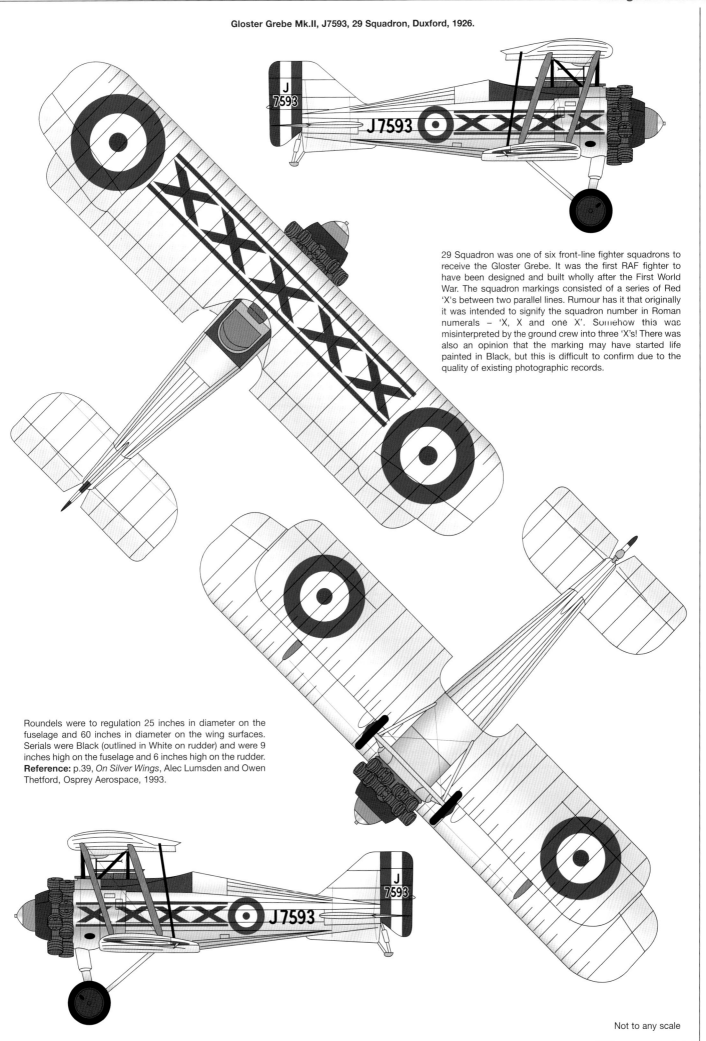

29 Squadron was one of six front-line fighter squadrons to receive the Gloster Grebe. It was the first RAF fighter to have been designed and built wholly after the First World War. The squadron markings consisted of a series of Red 'X's between two parallel lines. Rumour has it that originally it was intended to signify the squadron number in Roman numerals – 'X, X and one X'. Somehow this was misinterpreted by the ground crew into three 'X's! There was also an opinion that the marking may have started life painted in Black, but this is difficult to confirm due to the quality of existing photographic records.

Roundels were to regulation 25 inches in diameter on the fuselage and 60 inches in diameter on the wing surfaces. Serials were Black (outlined in White on rudder) and were 9 inches high on the fuselage and 6 inches high on the rudder.
Reference: p.39, *On Silver Wings*, Alec Lumsden and Owen Thetford, Osprey Aerospace, 1993.

Not to any scale

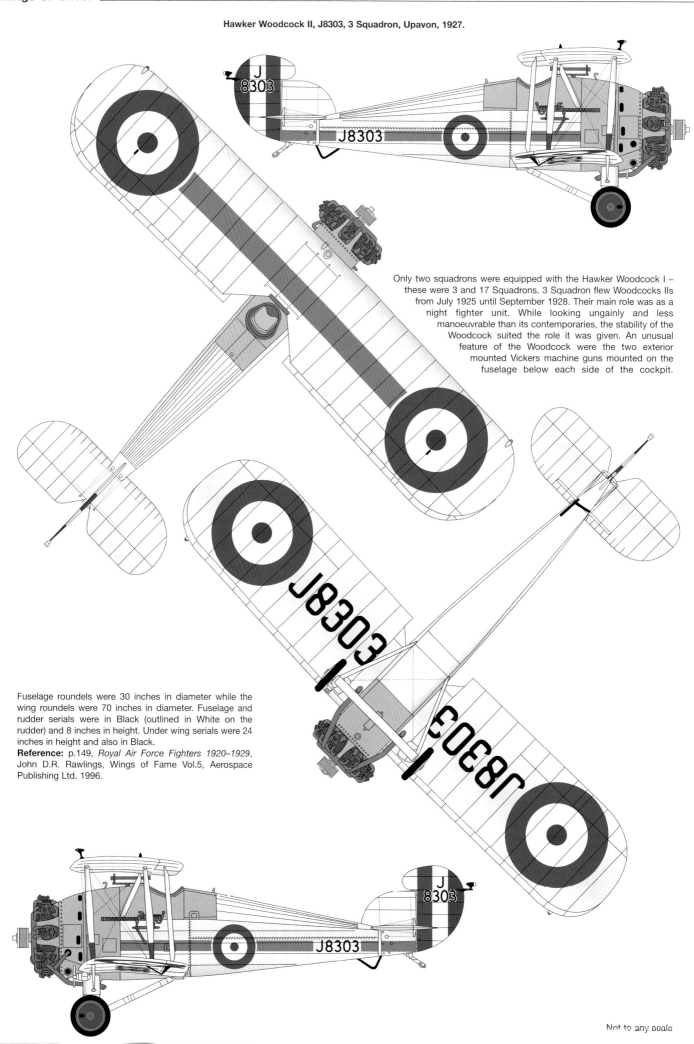

Hawker Woodcock II, J8303, 3 Squadron, Upavon, 1927.

Only two squadrons were equipped with the Hawker Woodcock I – these were 3 and 17 Squadrons. 3 Squadron flew Woodcocks IIs from July 1925 until September 1928. Their main role was as a night fighter unit. While looking ungainly and less manoeuvrable than its contemporaries, the stability of the Woodcock suited the role it was given. An unusual feature of the Woodcock were the two exterior mounted Vickers machine guns mounted on the fuselage below each side of the cockpit.

Fuselage roundels were 30 inches in diameter while the wing roundels were 70 inches in diameter. Fuselage and rudder serials were in Black (outlined in White on the rudder) and 8 inches in height. Under wing serials were 24 inches in height and also in Black.
Reference: p.149, *Royal Air Force Fighters 1920–1929*, John D.R. Rawlings, Wings of Fame Vol.5, Aerospace Publishing Ltd. 1996.

Not to any scale

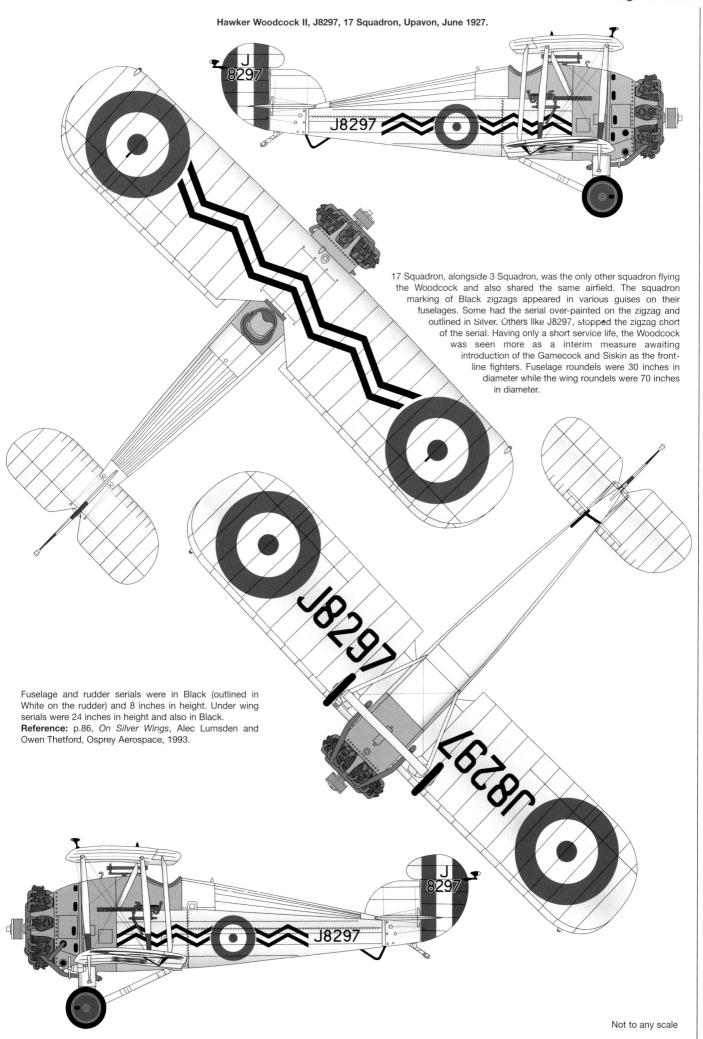

Hawker Woodcock II, J8297, 17 Squadron, Upavon, June 1927.

17 Squadron, alongside 3 Squadron, was the only other squadron flying the Woodcock and also shared the same airfield. The squadron marking of Black zigzags appeared in various guises on their fuselages. Some had the serial over-painted on the zigzag and outlined in Silver. Others like J8297, stopped the zigzag short of the serial. Having only a short service life, the Woodcock was seen more as a interim measure awaiting introduction of the Gamecock and Siskin as the front-line fighters. Fuselage roundels were 30 inches in diameter while the wing roundels were 70 inches in diameter.

Fuselage and rudder serials were in Black (outlined in White on the rudder) and 8 inches in height. Under wing serials were 24 inches in height and also in Black.
Reference: p.86, *On Silver Wings*, Alec Lumsden and Owen Thetford, Osprey Aerospace, 1993.

Not to any scale

Hawker Horsley Mk.II, S1443, 36 Squadron, Donibristle, October 1930.

The RAF's coastal defence Torpedo Flight was converted to 36 Squadron at Donibristle in October 1929. 36 Squadron's Horsleys were the first land-based RAF unit to take up the torpedo attack capability since the Sopwith Cuckoos of the First World War. S1443 was an all-metal Mk.II aircraft. No squadron markings were applied during this period apart from the large aircraft identification letter on the fuselage. Fuselage roundels were approximately 32 inches in diameter upper-wing roundels were approximately 100 inches in diameter and lower-wing roundels 60 inches in diameter. Fuselage and rudder serials were in Black, (outlined in White on rudder) and were 8 inches in height. Under-wing serials were also in Black and approximately 24 inches in height.

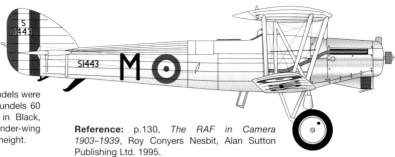

Reference: p.130, *The RAF in Camera 1903–1939*, Roy Conyers Nesbit, Alan Sutton Publishing Ltd. 1995.

Hawker Horsley Mk.II, S1243, 100 Squadron, Donibristle, 1930.

100 Squadron was converted from a day bomber squadron to a coastal defence squadron in 1930. It moved to Donibristle in Fifeshire to replace 36 Squadron who took up overseas duties in the Far East. Part of their new role included torpedo attacks and exercises with the Home Fleet. S1243 carried the squadron number in the flight colour and an individual aircraft number in White on a Blue band on the fuselage. A small 'unofficial' squadron badge appeared on the fin. Fuselage roundels were approximately 32 inches in diameter upper-wing roundels were approximately 100 inches in diameter and lower-wing roundels 60 inches in diameter. Fuselage and rudder serials were in Black, (outlined in White on rudder) and were 8 inches in height. Under-wing serials were also in Black and approximately 24 inches in height.

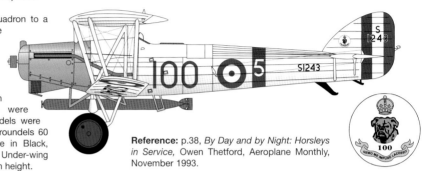

Reference: p.38, *By Day and by Night: Horsleys in Service,* Owen Thetford, Aeroplane Monthly, November 1993.

Hawker Horsley Mk.II, J8609, 504 (County of Nottingham) Special Reserve Squadron, Hucknall, 1932.

504 Squadron was formed at RAF Hucknall, Nottingham on 26 March 1928 as a Special Reserve Squadron. The squadron number in Red was positioned on the forward fuselage and a small squadron badge bearing the Nottingham coat of arms, appeared on the fin. Note the smaller 'doughnut' wheels on J8609 and 'Battleship Grey' metal panels. Fuselage roundels were approximately 32 inches in diameter, upper-wing roundels approximately 100 inches in diameter and lower-wing roundels 60 inches in diameter. Fuselage and rudder serials were in Black, (outlined in White on rudder) and were 8 inches in height. Under-wing serials were also in Black and approximately 24 inches in height.

Reference: p.27, *Memories of the Hawker Horsley*, Tommy Lucke, Aircraft Illustrated Extra No. 4, Ian Allan Ltd.

Hawker Horsley Mk.II, J8615, Gosport Development Flight, Gosport, October 1932.

The Horsley became an excellent 'test-bed' for the RAF to test various engines and armaments. J8615 was one of three aircraft detached to the Gosport Development Flight to test the Horsley's torpedo attack capabilities. It carried a Blue chevron on the fin and Red discs on the wheel covers. Fuselage roundels were approximately 32 inches in diameter, upper wing roundels were approximately 100 inches in diameter and lower wing roundels 60 inches in diameter. Fuselage and rudder serials were in Black (outlined in White on rudder) and were 8 inches in height. Under-wing serials were also in Black and approximately 24 inches in height.

Reference: p.33, *By Day and by Night: Horsleys in Service,* Owen Thetford, Aeroplane Monthly, November 1993.

Hawker Horsley Mk.II, S1452, 36 Squadron, Seletar, Singapore 1936.

S1452 displayed unusual markings and also a lack of national insignia! 36 Squadron were in Singapore from 1930 to 1935. Our reference is dated 1936 and so shows S1452 after retirement from front-line duties. Some aircraft were kept on as target tugs at Kai Tak, Hong Kong. This aircraft may have formed part of the Station Flight or commanding officer's runabout. Upper-wing roundels were approximately 100 inches in diameter and lower-wing roundels 60 inches in diameter. Fuselage serials were in Black, and 8 inches in height. Under wing serials were also in Black and approximately 24 inches in height.

Reference: p.35, *By Day and by Night: Horsleys in Service*, Owen Thetford, Aeroplane Monthly, November 1993.

Not to any scale

Armstrong Whitworth Siskin IIIA, J-8834, 1 Squadron, Tangmere, 1929. Pilot: Squadron Leader E.O. Grenfell.

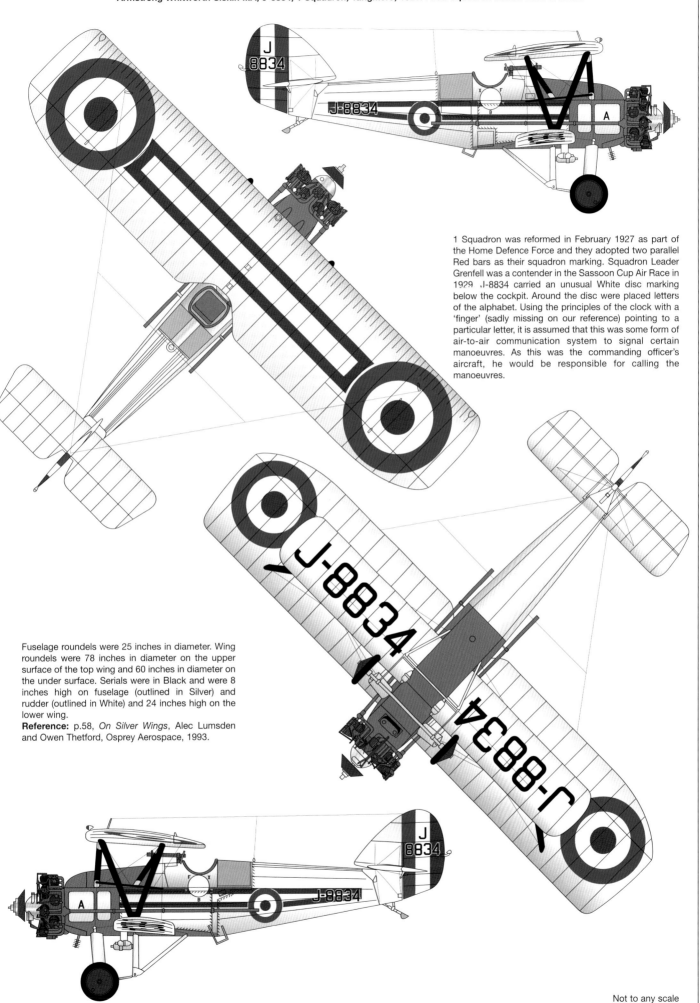

1 Squadron was reformed in February 1927 as part of the Home Defence Force and they adopted two parallel Red bars as their squadron marking. Squadron Leader Grenfell was a contender in the Sassoon Cup Air Race in 1929. J-8834 carried an unusual White disc marking below the cockpit. Around the disc were placed letters of the alphabet. Using the principles of the clock with a 'finger' (sadly missing on our reference) pointing to a particular letter, it is assumed that this was some form of air-to-air communication system to signal certain manoeuvres. As this was the commanding officer's aircraft, he would be responsible for calling the manoeuvres.

Fuselage roundels were 25 inches in diameter. Wing roundels were 78 inches in diameter on the upper surface of the top wing and 60 inches in diameter on the under surface. Serials were in Black and were 8 inches high on fuselage (outlined in Silver) and rudder (outlined in White) and 24 inches high on the lower wing.
Reference: p.58, *On Silver Wings*, Alec Lumsden and Owen Thetford, Osprey Aerospace, 1993.

Not to any scale

Armstrong Whitworth Siskin III, J-7760, 41 Squadron, Northolt, 1926.

41 Squadron and 111 Squadron were the only two squadrons to use the Siskin III. The Siskin III's distinguishing features were a deeper rudder and auxiliary fin below the rear fuselage and a greater dihedral on the top wing. Fuselage roundels were 25 inches in diameter. Wing roundels were 78 inches on the upper surface and 60 inches on the under surface of the top wing. Serials were 8 inches high in Black with Silver outline on the fuselage and Black with White outline on the rudder. Under-wing serials were also Black and 24 inches in height.

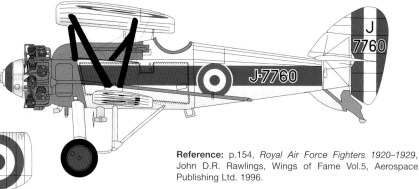

Reference: p.154, *Royal Air Force Fighters 1920–1929*, John D.R. Rawlings, Wings of Fame Vol.5, Aerospace Publishing Ltd. 1996.

Armstrong Whitworth Siskin IIIDC, J-7549, 111 Squadron, Duxford, 1928.

Each Siskin squadron was allocated at least one dual-control, two-seat trainer. Most of these were converted Siskin IIIs. The squadron marking of a thin Black band along the fuselage and across the top wing was later thickened on the Siskin IIIAs. Fuselage roundels were 25 inches in diameter. Wing roundels were 78 inches on the upper surface and 60 inches on the under surface of the top wing. Serials were 8 inches high in Black on both fuselage and rudder (White outline on the rudder). Under-wing serials were also Black and 24 inches in height.

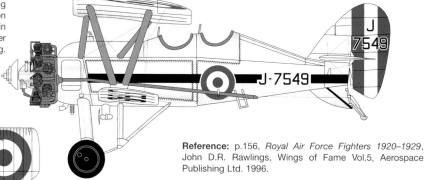

Reference: p.156, *Royal Air Force Fighters 1920–1929*, John D.R. Rawlings, Wings of Fame Vol.5, Aerospace Publishing Ltd. 1996.

Armstrong Whitworth Siskin IIIDC, J-8646, 41 Squadron, Northolt, 1928.

41 Squadron was the first squadron to upgrade to the Siskin IIIA in 1927. Notable on this aircraft was another example of the 'letter clock' below the pilot's cockpit. This example clearly shows the 'clock' finger pointing to one of the six letter codes on the face. Unfortunately, reference does not verify if this feature was repeated on the starboard side. If, as we expect, this was some form of manoeuvre-signalling device, a similar, mirrored, image would be displayed. Fuselage roundels were 25 inches in diameter. Wing roundels were 78 inches on the upper surface and 60 inches on the under surface of the top wing. Serials were 8 inches high in Silver on the fuselage and Black outlined in White on the rudder. Under-wing serials were also Black and 24 inches in height.

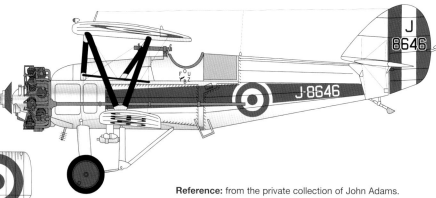

Reference: from the private collection of John Adams.

Armstrong Whitworth Siskin IIIA, J-8950, 29 Squadron, Duxford, 1929.

J-8950 was built by Gloster Aircraft. Note the typical Gloster font style on the serials. The squadron marking was reduced to three Red X's on the fuselage and six on the upper wing. Fuselage roundels were 25 inches in diameter. Wing roundels were 78 inches on the upper surface and 60 inches on the under surface of the top wing. Serials were 8 inches high in Black on both fuselage and rudder (White outline on the rudder). Under-wing serials were also Black and 24 inches in height.

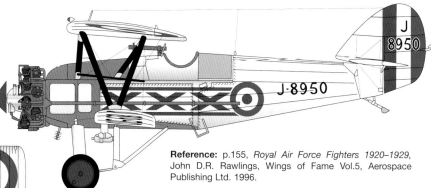

Reference: p.155, *Royal Air Force Fighters 1920–1929*, John D.R. Rawlings, Wings of Fame Vol.5, Aerospace Publishing Ltd. 1996.

Not to any scale

Armstrong Whitworth Siskin IIIA, J-8959, 43 Squadron, Tangmere, 1930. Pilot: Squadron Leader C.N. Lowe, MC DFC.

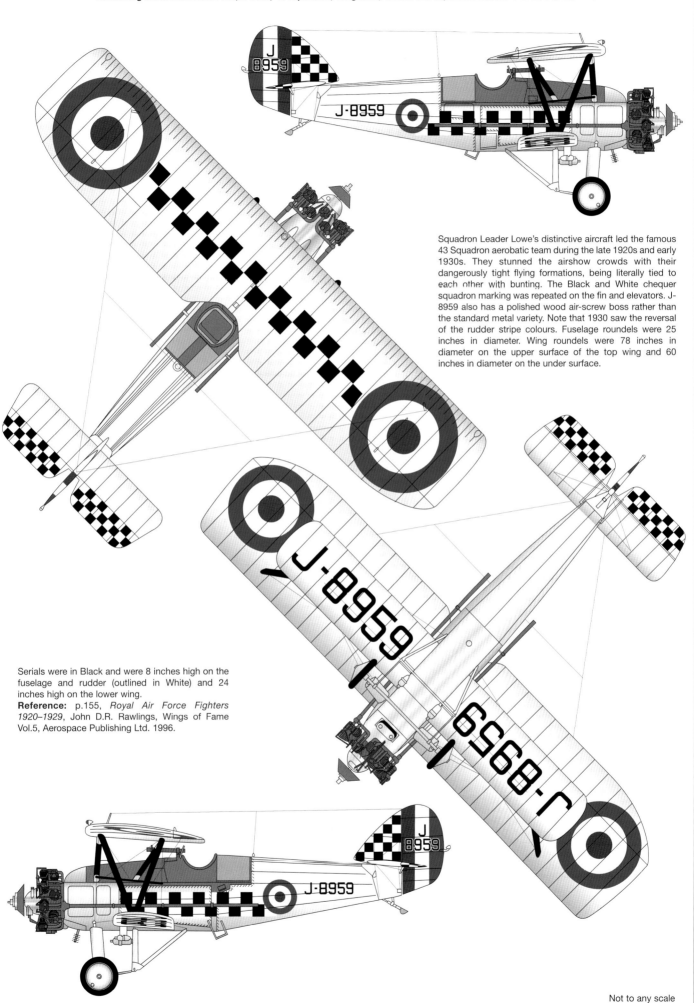

Squadron Leader Lowe's distinctive aircraft led the famous 43 Squadron aerobatic team during the late 1920s and early 1930s. They stunned the airshow crowds with their dangerously tight flying formations, being literally tied to each other with bunting. The Black and White chequer squadron marking was repeated on the fin and elevators. J-8959 also has a polished wood air-screw boss rather than the standard metal variety. Note that 1930 saw the reversal of the rudder stripe colours. Fuselage roundels were 25 inches in diameter. Wing roundels were 78 inches in diameter on the upper surface of the top wing and 60 inches in diameter on the under surface.

Serials were in Black and were 8 inches high on the fuselage and rudder (outlined in White) and 24 inches high on the lower wing.
Reference: p.155, *Royal Air Force Fighters 1920–1929*, John D.R. Rawlings, Wings of Fame Vol.5, Aerospace Publishing Ltd. 1996.

Not to any scale

Armstrong Whitworth Siskin IIIA, J-8386, 41 Squadron, Northolt, May 1927. Pilot: Flying Officer H.T. Andrews.

Flying Officer Andrews used this aircraft to compete in the Sir Philip Sassoon Cup at RAF Northolt on 26 May 1927. The 100 mile circular course took the competitors around Northolt, Duxford and Halton. Flying Officer Andrews averaged 142 mph and finished fourth in the race. J-8386 carried some unusual modifications. Note the shorter exhaust and revised foot steps. Also the extra engine cowl to improve aerodynamics. Note also the small aircraft identification letter in White on the nose panel. Fuselage roundels were 25 inches in diameter. Wing roundels were 78 inches in diameter on the upper surface of the top wing and 60 inches in diameter on the under surface. Serials were in Black and were 8 inches high on fuselage (outlined in Silver) and rudder (outlined in White) and 24 inches high on the lower wing.

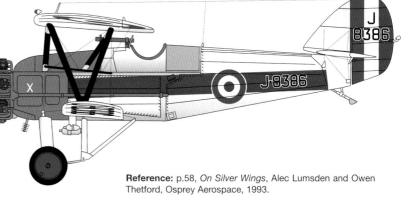

Reference: p.58, *On Silver Wings*, Alec Lumsden and Owen Thetford, Osprey Aerospace, 1993.

Armstrong Whitworth Siskin IIIA, J-8394, 43 Squadron, Tangmere, 1929.

43 Squadron received their first Siskins in 1928, flying them until the arrival of the Fury in 1931. J-8394 was an early IIIA production type with standard Nivo Green finish to forward fuselage and undercarriage struts. Note also the natural metal cowl behind the propeller boss, lack of stirrup type foot step and aircraft identification letter on the engine panel. Fuselage roundels were 25 inches in diameter. Wing roundels were 78 inches on the upper surface and 60 inches on the under surface of the top wing. Serials were 8 inches high in Black on both fuselage and rudder (White outline on the rudder). Under-wing serials were also Black and 24 inches in height.

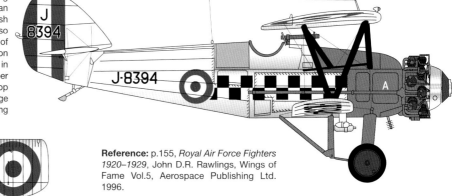

Reference: p.155, *Royal Air Force Fighters 1920–1929*, John D.R. Rawlings, Wings of Fame Vol.5, Aerospace Publishing Ltd. 1996.

Armstrong Whitworth Siskin IIIA, J-9901, 19 Squadron, Duxford, 1930.

The Blue and White chequer squadron markings of 19 Squadron were noticeably bigger on the fuselage than their fellow chequer squadrons, 43 and 56. However, on the upper-wing the sizes were similar apart from being in reverse order. Fuselage roundels were 25 inches in diameter. Wing roundels were 78 inches on the upper surface and 60 inches on the under surface of the top wing. Serials were 8 inches high in Black on both fuselage and rudder (White outline on the rudder). Under-wing serials were also Black and 24 inches in height.

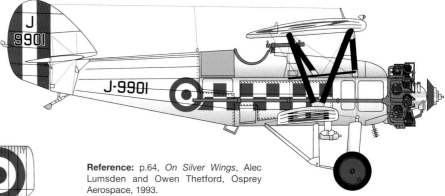

Reference: p.64, *On Silver Wings*, Alec Lumsden and Owen Thetford, Osprey Aerospace, 1993.

Armstrong Whitworth Siskin IIIA, J-9895, 56 Squadron, North Weald, 1930.

By 1930, 56 Squadron's markings had become more simplified with fewer Red and White chequers on the fuselage. Note that the AMO (Air Ministry Order) of 1930 had brought in the reversal of the rudder stripe colours. Note also the Silver painted covers on the radio compartment. Fuselage roundels were 25 inches in diameter. Wing roundels were 78 inches on the upper surface and 60 inches on the under surface of the top wing. Serials were 8 inches high in Black on both fuselage and rudder (White outline on the rudder). Under-wing serials were also Black and 24 inches in height.

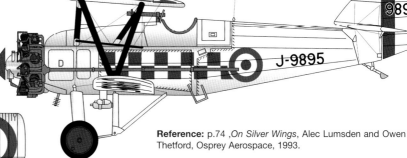

Reference: p.74, *On Silver Wings*, Alec Lumsden and Owen Thetford, Osprey Aerospace, 1993.

Not to any scale

Armstrong Whitworth Siskin IIIA J-8934. 56 Squadron, North Weald, 1930

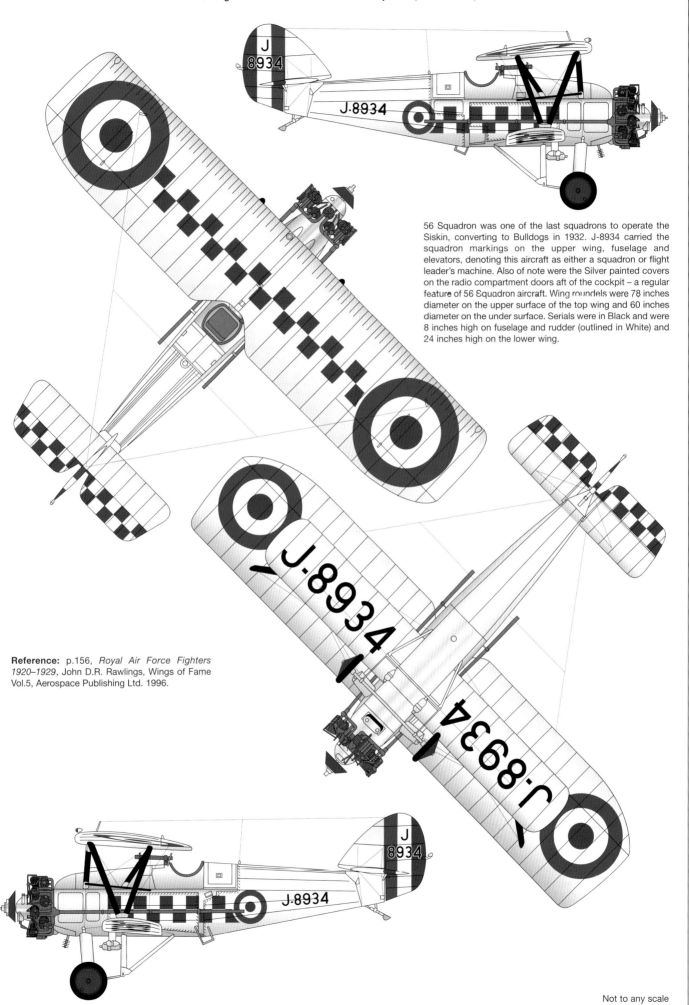

56 Squadron was one of the last squadrons to operate the Siskin, converting to Bulldogs in 1932. J-8934 carried the squadron markings on the upper wing, fuselage and elevators, denoting this aircraft as either a squadron or flight leader's machine. Also of note were the Silver painted covers on the radio compartment doors aft of the cockpit – a regular feature of 56 Squadron aircraft. Wing roundels were 78 inches diameter on the upper surface of the top wing and 60 inches diameter on the under surface. Serials were in Black and were 8 inches high on fuselage and rudder (outlined in White) and 24 inches high on the lower wing.

Reference: p.156, *Royal Air Force Fighters 1920–1929*, John D.R. Rawlings, Wings of Fame Vol.5, Aerospace Publishing Ltd. 1996.

Not to any scale

Fairey Fawn Mk.II, J7209, 100 Squadron, Spitalgate, 1925.

The Fairey Fawn was the first day bomber designed in the 1920s. It was intended to replace the DH.9A, but in many respects it was inferior in both performance and suitability. Its inability to be deployed overseas resulted in the DH.9A having to soldier on until the Wapiti was fully developed. 100 Squadron was one of the first three squadrons to receive the Fawn and is shown here as it appeared at the RAF Hendon Air Display in 1925. The number indicates the individual aircraft number. Fuselage roundels were approximately 28 inches in diameter, while the wing roundels were 70 inches in diameter. Serials were in Black and 8 inches in height on fuselage and rudder (outlined in White on the rudder).

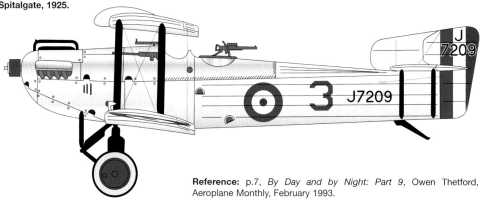

Reference: p.7, *By Day and by Night: Part 9*, Owen Thetford, Aeroplane Monthly, February 1993.

Fairey Fawn Mk.II, J7212, 12 Squadron, Andover, 1926.

12 Squadron was one of the first squadrons to receive the Fawn and, frustratingly for the pilots, one of the last to relinquish them! Fortunately they were the squadron chosen to be replaced with the revolutionary new Fairey Fox in December 1926. No squadron markings were applied apart from the small-encircled '12' on the fin. Fuselage roundels were approximately 28 inches in diameter, while the wing roundels were 70 inches in diameter. Serials were in Black and 8 inches in height on fuselage and rudder (outlined in White on the rudder).

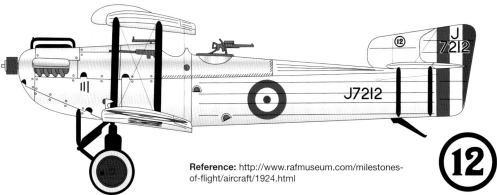

Reference: http://www.rafmuseum.com/milestones-of-flight/aircraft/1924.html

Fairey Fawn Mk.II, J7190, 602 (City of Glasgow) Squadron, Royal Auxiliary Air Force, Renfrew, 1928.

602 Squadron received their Fawns in September 1927. They met with little enthusiasm from the squadron's pilots. One is quoted as saying, "It had the aerodynamic qualities of a half-brick". It is thought that the Red bars either side of the fuselage roundel were an early experiment in squadron markings. J7190 also carried an individual aircraft identification number '2' on the fuselage below the centre section struts. Fuselage roundels were approximately 28 inches in diameter, while the wing roundels were 70 inches in diameter. Serials were in Black and 8 inches in height on the fuselage and rudder (outlined in White on the rudder).

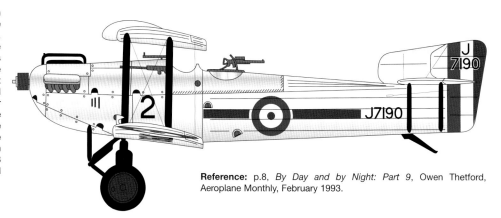

Reference: p.8, *By Day and by Night: Part 9*, Owen Thetford, Aeroplane Monthly, February 1993.

Fairey Fawn Mk.II, J7206, 503 (County of Lincoln) Special Reserve Squadron, Waddington, 1928.

As was the custom, the part-time pilots of 503 Special Reserve Squadron received their Fawns as they were handed over by the regular RAF units. They flew the Fawn until February 1929 when they went over to night-bomber duties with Handley Page Hyderabads. Officially, 503 Squadron was not recognised as having squadron markings, however J7206 clearly showed the Blue and Red fuselage bands illustrated. Fuselage roundels were approximately 28 inches in diameter, while the wing roundels were 70 inches in diameter. Serials were in Black and 8 inches in height on the fuselage and rudder (outlined in white on the rudder).

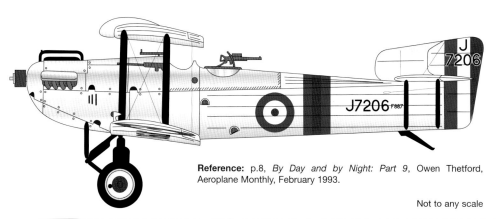

Reference: p.8, *By Day and by Night: Part 9*, Owen Thetford, Aeroplane Monthly, February 1993.

Not to any scale

Fairey IIIF Mk.IV M/A, J9796, 47 Squadron, Khartoum, Egypt 1928.

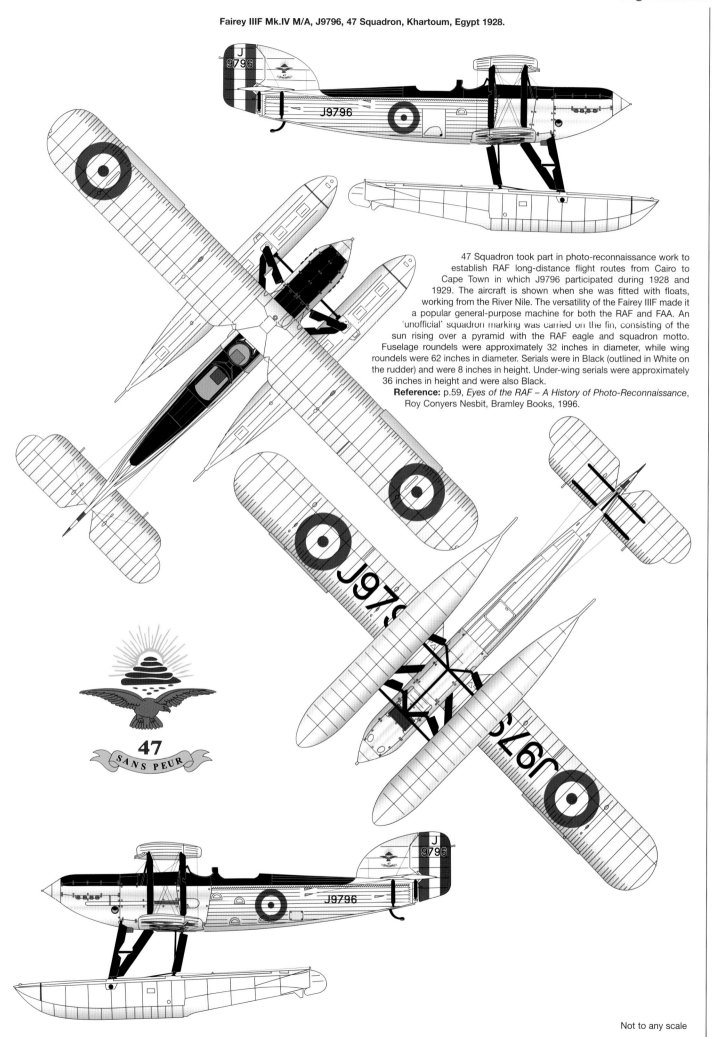

47 Squadron took part in photo-reconnaissance work to establish RAF long-distance flight routes from Cairo to Cape Town in which J9796 participated during 1928 and 1929. The aircraft is shown when she was fitted with floats, working from the River Nile. The versatility of the Fairey IIIF made it a popular general-purpose machine for both the RAF and FAA. An 'unofficial' squadron marking was carried on the fin, consisting of the sun rising over a pyramid with the RAF eagle and squadron motto. Fuselage roundels were approximately 32 inches in diameter, while wing roundels were 62 inches in diameter. Serials were in Black (outlined in White on the rudder) and were 8 inches in height. Under-wing serials were approximately 36 inches in height and were also Black.

Reference: p.59, *Eyes of the RAF – A History of Photo-Reconnaissance*, Roy Conyers Nesbit, Bramley Books, 1996.

47
SANS PEUR

Not to any scale

Fairey IIIF Mk.III, S1141, 47 Squadron, Commander's aircraft, Khartoum, Sudan, 1929.

S1141 was an early pre-production batch of ten Fairey IIIDs which were modified to IIIFs on the production line. It displayed the more angular early fin design. This aircraft made one of the long-distance Cairo to Cape Town training flights. These long-distance flights were pioneered by the RAF in Africa and did much to 'show the flag' to the colonies of the Empire. Fuselage roundels were approximately 32 inches in diameter. Wing roundels were approximately 62 inches in diameter. Serials on the fuselage and rudder were Black outlined in White and were 8 inches in height. Under-wing serials were approximately 36 inches in height, also in Black.

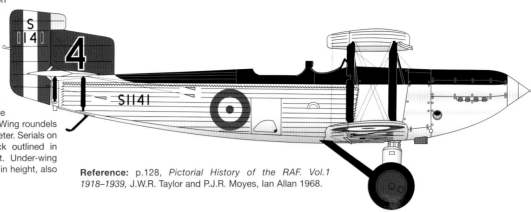

Reference: p.128, *Pictorial History of the RAF. Vol.1 1918–1939*, J.W.R. Taylor and P.J.R. Moyes, Ian Allan 1968.

Fairey IIIF Mk.IVM/A, K1115, 24 Squadron (Communications) Royal Flight, Kenley 1930.

Although part of 24 Squadron, K1115 was designated part of the King's Royal Flight. While Prince of Wales, the later King Edward VIII, flew regularly in the Fairey IIIF, a Bristol F.2B and Westland Wapiti. This formed the nucleus of what was to become the Royal Flight, officially established in 1936. Note the converted rear cockpit area and added windshield. K1115 carried both the 24 Squadron number in Red on the fuselage and the Royal Flight Red chevron on the fin. Fuselage roundels were approximately 32 inches in diameter and the wing roundels 62 inches in diameter. Serials were 8 inches in height on both fuselage and rudder and were Black outlined in White. Under-wing serials were also in Black and approximately 36 inches in height.

Reference: p.34, *By Day and by Night – Fairey IIIF and Gordon in Service*, Owen Thetford, Aeroplane Monthly, May 1994.

Fairey IIIF Mk.I, S1172, 45 Squadron, Helwan, Egypt, 1930.

45 Squadron was based in Egypt from 1929 to 1935. As well as Helwan, various detachments were, at times, deployed to Gaza, Ismailia and Iraq. S1172 was a Mk.I machine and is shown with the early fin design. Fuselage roundels were approximately 32 inches in diameter. Wing roundels were approximately 62 inches in diameter. Serials on the fuselage and rudder were Black outlined in White and were 8 inches in height. Under-wing serials were approximately 36 inches in height, also in Black.

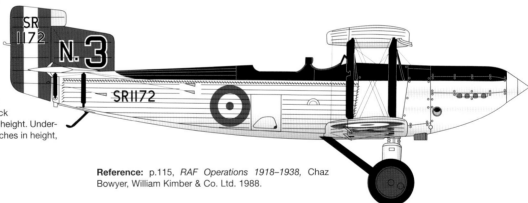

Reference: p.115, *RAF Operations 1918–1938*, Chaz Bowyer, William Kimber & Co. Ltd. 1988.

Fairey IIIF Mk.IVM/A, J9675, 8 Squadron, B Flight, Khormaksar, Aden, June 1931.

8 Squadron was based in Aden from 1929 to 1935. The squadron's main role was in supporting ground forces quelling rebel tribesmen. 'Demonstration' flights and leaflet dropping were the preferred methods of calming the rebels, but inevitably and as a last resort, bombing and strafing operations were carried out. Individual aircraft letters on the fin were the only squadron markings during this period. Fuselage roundels were approximately 32 inches in diameter. Wing roundels were approximately 62 inches in diameter. Serials on the fuselage and rudder were Black (outlined in White on the rudder) and were 8 inches in height. Under-wing serials were approximately 36 inches in height, also in Black.

Reference: p.38, *By Day and by Night – Fairey IIIF and Gordon in Service*, Owen Thetford, Aeroplane Monthly, May 1994.

Not to any scale

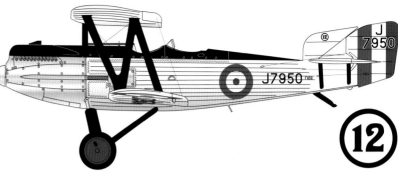

Fairey Fox I, J7950, 12 Squadron, Andover, 1928.

C.R. Fairey, the designer of the Fox, was inspired by the Curtiss CR-3 seaplane which won the 1923 Schneider Trophy. Initially, Fairey built the Fox independently without RAF specification. Its capabilities as a light daylight bomber exceeded anything that was in service with the RAF at that time. The RAF recognised its outstanding qualities and ordered eighteen aircraft. These were allocated to 12 Squadron which became the only squadron to fly the Fox. At the time, its design was revolutionary and set standards for future light bomber design specifications for the RAF. Note the 12 Squadron marking on the fin and small factory number after the serial. Fuselage roundels were approximately 28 inches in diameter and wing roundels 62 inches in diameter. Serials were Black, outlined in White on both fuselage and rudder and were 8 inches in height. Under-wing serials were also Black and approximately 24 inches in height.

Reference: p.8, *Fairey's Elusive Fox*, Ian Huntley, Aeroplane Monthly, January 1979.

Fairey Fox IA, J7949, 12 Squadron, Andover, 1930.

The Rolls-Royce Kestrel engine further streamlined the elegant Fox IA and increased its top speed to 167mph. Embarrassingly for the fighter arm of the RAF, it became a bomber which could outpace them! 12 Squadron were so taken by the Fox that they adopted a fox's head as their squadron emblem. This was ringed by the flight colour and on top, the Roman numeral 'XII'. J7949 is shown with its retractable chin radiator extended. Armament consisted of a fixed 0.303-inch Vickers machine gun on the port side fuselage and a high-speed mounted 0.303-inch Lewis gun in the rear cockpit. This could be stored away or set for firing downwards through a hatch in the rear cockpit floor. Fuselage roundels were approximately 28 inches in diameter and wing roundels 62 inches in diameter. Serials were Black, outlined in White on both fuselage and rudder and were 8 inches in height. Under-wing serials were also Black and approximately 24 inches in height.
Reference: p.33, *Fox in Service*, Owen Thetford, Aeroplane Monthly, February 1994.

Fairey Gordon, K1736, 40 Squadron, Upper Heyford, 1932. Pilot: Squadron Leader Malcolm Taylor.

The squadron number was prominently displayed below the observer's cockpit in the Flight colour and the unit's badge appears on the fin. Fuselage roundels were approximately 32 inches in diameter. Wing roundels were approximately 62 inches in diameter. Serials on fuselage and rudder were in Black, (outlined in White on the rudder), and were 8 inches in height. Under-wing serials were approximately 36 inches in height, also in Black.
Reference: p.17, *Fairey IIIF and Gordon in Service*, Owen Thetford, Aeroplane Monthly, June 1994.

Fairey Gordon, K2617, 6 Squadron, Ismailia, Egypt, 1932.

6 Squadron was based in Egypt from June 1931 until October 1935 with detachments in Palestine. K2617 displays the squadron badge on its fin over a diagonal 'gunner's stripe'. The Red fin signifying this was either the commander's or flight leader's aircraft. Fuselage roundels were approximately 32 inches in diameter. Wing roundels were approximately 62 inches in diameter. Fuselage and rudder serials were Black (outlined in White on the rudder) and were 8 inches in height. Under-wing serials were approximately 36 inches in height, also in Black.

Reference: p.72, *Aircraft Camouflage and Markings 1907–1954*, Bruce Robertson, Harleyford Publications Limited, 1956.

Fairey Gordon, K1776, 35 Squadron, Bircham Newton (Norfolk), 1934.

K1776 was one of six converted Fairey IIIFs allocated to 35 Squadron. The individual aircraft identity number was positioned on the forward fuselage panels in the flight colour. The squadron number, again in the flight colour, appeared prominently below the pilot's cockpit. Fuselage roundels were approximately 32 inches in diameter. Wing roundels were approximately 62 inches in diameter. Serials on the fuselage and rudder were Black (outlined in White on the rudder) and were 8 inches in height. Under-wing serials were approximately 36 inches in height, also in Black.

Reference: p.64, *Eyes of the RAF*, Roy Conyers Nesbit, Bramley Books, 1997.

Not to any scale

Gloster Gamecock I, J8084, 23 Squadron, Henlow 1927. Pilot: Squadron Leader Raymond Collishaw, DSO OBE DSC DFC.

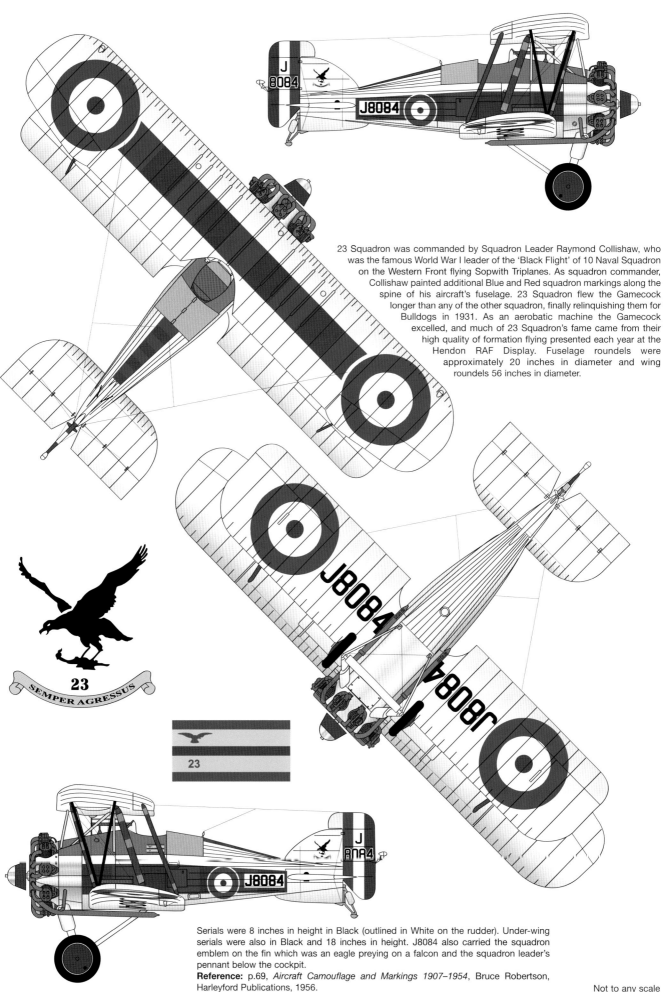

23 Squadron was commanded by Squadron Leader Raymond Collishaw, who was the famous World War I leader of the 'Black Flight' of 10 Naval Squadron on the Western Front flying Sopwith Triplanes. As squadron commander, Collishaw painted additional Blue and Red squadron markings along the spine of his aircraft's fuselage. 23 Squadron flew the Gamecock longer than any of the other squadron, finally relinquishing them for Bulldogs in 1931. As an aerobatic machine the Gamecock excelled, and much of 23 Squadron's fame came from their high quality of formation flying presented each year at the Hendon RAF Display. Fuselage roundels were approximately 20 inches in diameter and wing roundels 56 inches in diameter.

Serials were 8 inches in height in Black (outlined in White on the rudder). Under-wing serials were also in Black and 18 inches in height. J8084 also carried the squadron emblem on the fin which was an eagle preying on a falcon and the squadron leader's pennant below the cockpit.

Reference: p.69, *Aircraft Camouflage and Markings 1907–1954*, Bruce Robertson, Harleyford Publications, 1956.

Not to any scale

Gloster Gamecock I, J8081, 32 Squadron, Kenley 1928.

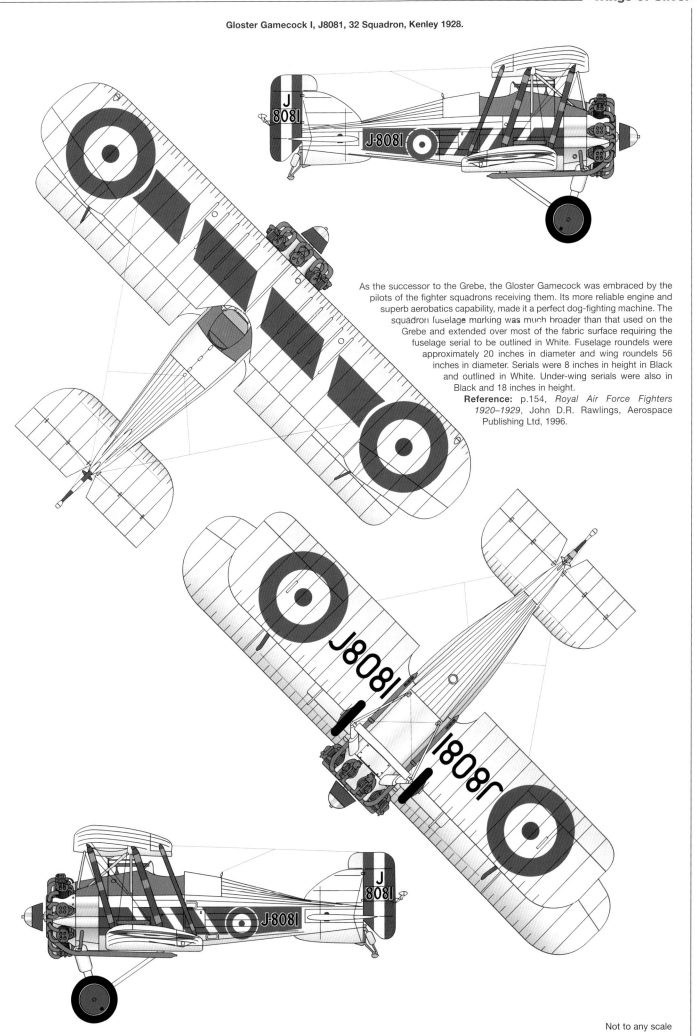

As the successor to the Grebe, the Gloster Gamecock was embraced by the pilots of the fighter squadrons receiving them. Its more reliable engine and superb aerobatics capability, made it a perfect dog-fighting machine. The squadron fuselage marking was much broader than that used on the Grebe and extended over most of the fabric surface requiring the fuselage serial to be outlined in White. Fuselage roundels were approximately 20 inches in diameter and wing roundels 56 inches in diameter. Serials were 8 inches in height in Black and outlined in White. Under-wing serials were also in Black and 18 inches in height.

Reference: p.154, *Royal Air Force Fighters 1920–1929*, John D.R. Rawlings, Aerospace Publishing Ltd, 1996.

Not to any scale

Gloster Gamecock I, J8090, 43 Squadron, Flight Commander's aircraft, Tangmere, 1928.

43 Squadron was one of the first squadrons to be re-equipped with the Gamecock after flying the long-obsolete Sopwith Snipe. It was around this time that the Air Ministry was encouraging squadrons to devise badges and mottos for their units and it was the Gamecock that inspired the name 'The Fighting Cocks' for 43 Squadron. This was also the period when the Black and White chequer markings were first introduced. Fuselage roundels were approximately 20 inches in diameter and wing roundels 56 inches in diameter. Serials were 8 inches in height in Black (outlined in White on the rudder). Under-wing serials were also in Black and 18 inches in height.
Reference: p.109, *On Silver Wings*, Alec Lumsden and Owen Thetford, Osprey Aerospace, 1993.

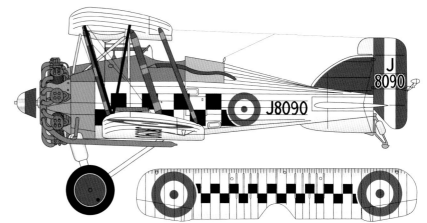

Gloster Gamecock I, J8081, 32 Squadron, Kenley 1928.

32 Squadron flew Gamecocks from September 1926 until April 1928. They were another unit famous for their aerobatic displays and regular entries in the annual RAF air race the Sassoon Cup. In 1927, it was won by a Gamecock of 32 Squadron with Gamecocks taking all three top places. The short length of the fuselage cramped the style of the squadron markings for most of the Gamecock units. 32 Squadron limited to three diagonals in the Blue band forward of the roundel. Fuselage roundels were approximately 20 inches in diameter and wing roundels 56 inches in diameter. Serials were 8 inches in height in Black (outlined in Silver on the fuselage and White on the rudder). Under-wing serials were also in Black and 18 inches in height.
Reference: p.154, *Royal Air Force Fighters 1920–1929*, John D.R. Rawlings, Aerospace Publishing Ltd, 1996.

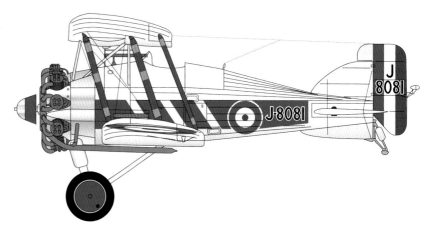

Gloster Gamecock I, J8089, Central Flying School, Upavon, 1929.

Unlike its contemporary the Grebe, the Gamecock saw relatively little service in the flying training role. Only one Gamecock was built in a two-seat configuration. Altogether six other Gamecocks were on the strength of the Central Flying School. Most of these being handed on from front line squadron service. No particular markings were evident at this time apart from the Central Flying School initials on the fin. Like many other Gamecocks, J8089 has been retro-fitted with additional inter-plane 'vee' struts to counter the aircraft's notorious wing flutter problem. Fuselage roundels were approximately 20 inches in diameter and wing roundels 56 inches in diameter. Serials were 8 inches in height in Black (outlined in White on the rudder). Under-wing serials were also in Black and 18 inches in height.
Reference: p.99, *On Silver Wings*, Alec Lumsden and Owen Thetford, Osprey Aerospace, 1993.

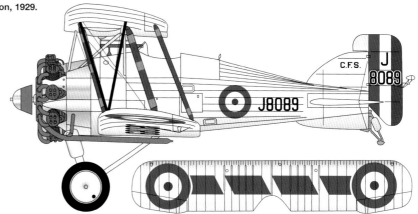

Gloster Gamecock I, J8470, 3 Squadron, Upavon, 1929.

3 Squadron shared the night fighter role with 17 Squadron and also shared the same aerodrome at Upavon. Its short service career of only ten months was really only a stand-in role to replace the problematic Hawker Woodcock until the new Bristol Bulldog was available. The squadron markings, of a Green band along the fuselage and top wing, was again rather abbreviated due to the short length of the aircraft. Fuselage roundels were approximately 20 inches in diameter and wing roundels 56 inches in diameter. Serials were 8 inches in height in Black (outlined in Silver on the fuselage and White on the rudder). Under-wing serials were also in Black and 18 inches in height.
Reference: p.159, *RAF Fighters 1920–1929*, John D.R. Rawlings, Wings of Fame Vol.5, Aerospace Publishing Ltd, 1996.

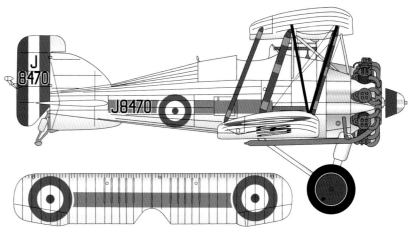

Not to any scale

Gloster Gamecock I, J8408, 17 Squadron, Upavon, 1928. Pilot: Squadron Leader A.R. Arnold, DSO DFC.

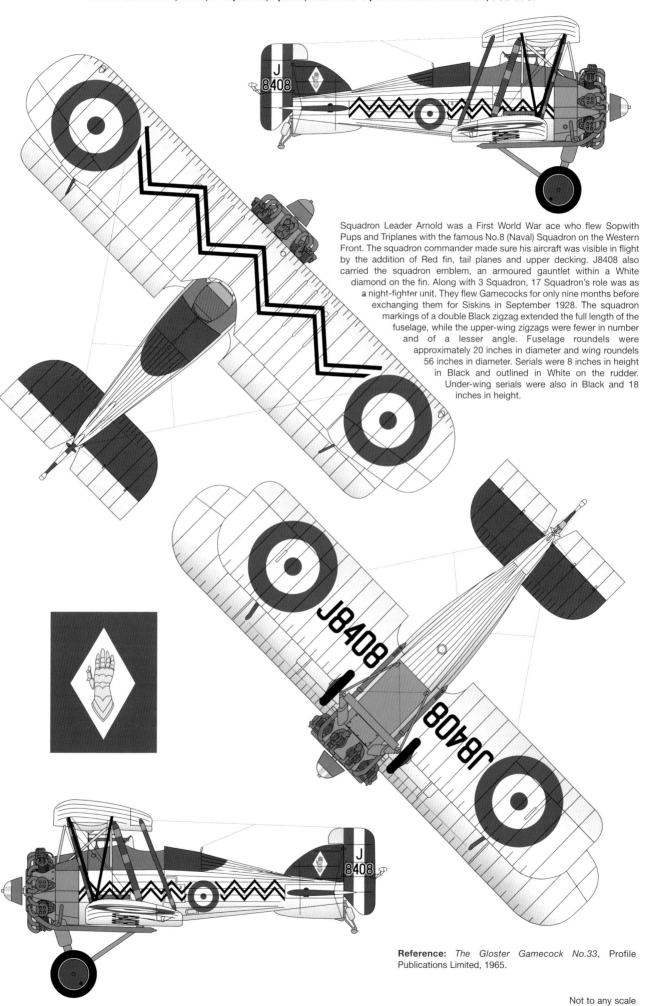

Squadron Leader Arnold was a First World War ace who flew Sopwith Pups and Triplanes with the famous No.8 (Naval) Squadron on the Western Front. The squadron commander made sure his aircraft was visible in flight by the addition of Red fin, tail planes and upper decking. J8408 also carried the squadron emblem, an armoured gauntlet within a White diamond on the fin. Along with 3 Squadron, 17 Squadron's role was as a night-fighter unit. They flew Gamecocks for only nine months before exchanging them for Siskins in September 1928. The squadron markings of a double Black zigzag extended the full length of the fuselage, while the upper-wing zigzags were fewer in number and of a lesser angle. Fuselage roundels were approximately 20 inches in diameter and wing roundels 56 inches in diameter. Serials were 8 inches in height in Black and outlined in White on the rudder. Under-wing serials were also in Black and 18 inches in height.

Reference: *The Gloster Gamecock No.33*, Profile Publications Limited, 1965.

Not to any scale

Bristol Bulldog Mk.II, J9574, 3 Squadron, Upavon, 1929.

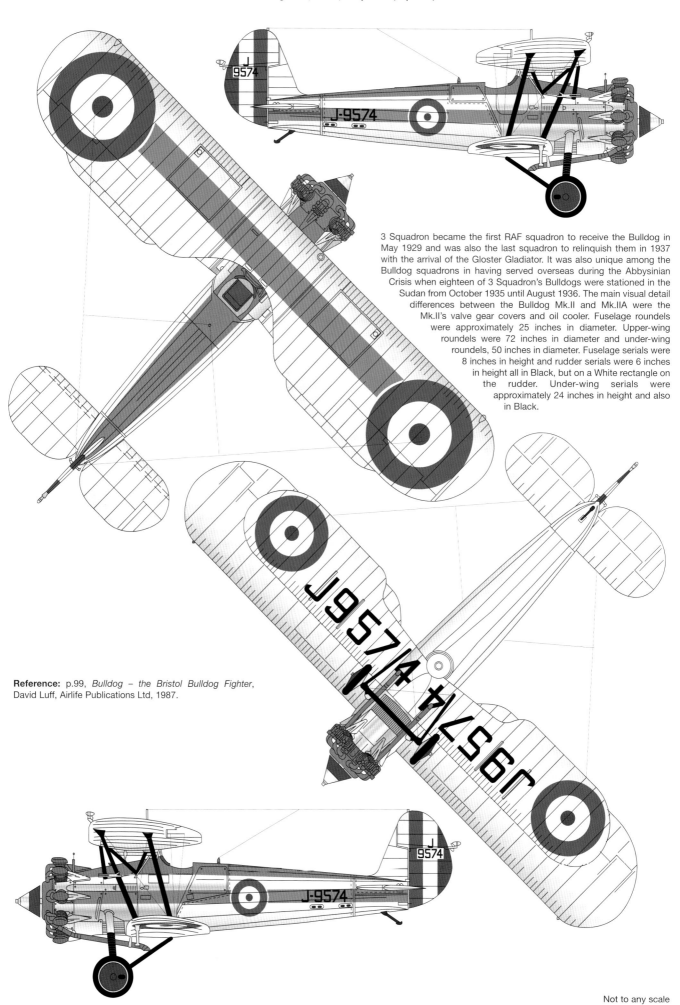

3 Squadron became the first RAF squadron to receive the Bulldog in May 1929 and was also the last squadron to relinquish them in 1937 with the arrival of the Gloster Gladiator. It was also unique among the Bulldog squadrons in having served overseas during the Abbysinian Crisis when eighteen of 3 Squadron's Bulldogs were stationed in the Sudan from October 1935 until August 1936. The main visual detail differences between the Bulldog Mk.II and Mk.IIA were the Mk.II's valve gear covers and oil cooler. Fuselage roundels were approximately 25 inches in diameter. Upper-wing roundels were 72 inches in diameter and under-wing roundels, 50 inches in diameter. Fuselage serials were 8 inches in height and rudder serials were 6 inches in height all in Black, but on a White rectangle on the rudder. Under-wing serials were approximately 24 inches in height and also in Black.

Reference: p.99, *Bulldog – the Bristol Bulldog Fighter*, David Luff, Airlife Publications Ltd, 1987.

Not to any scale

Bristol Bulldog Mk.IIa, K2159, 19 Squadron, Duxford, 1931. Pilot: Squadron Leader A.C. Sanderson, DFC.

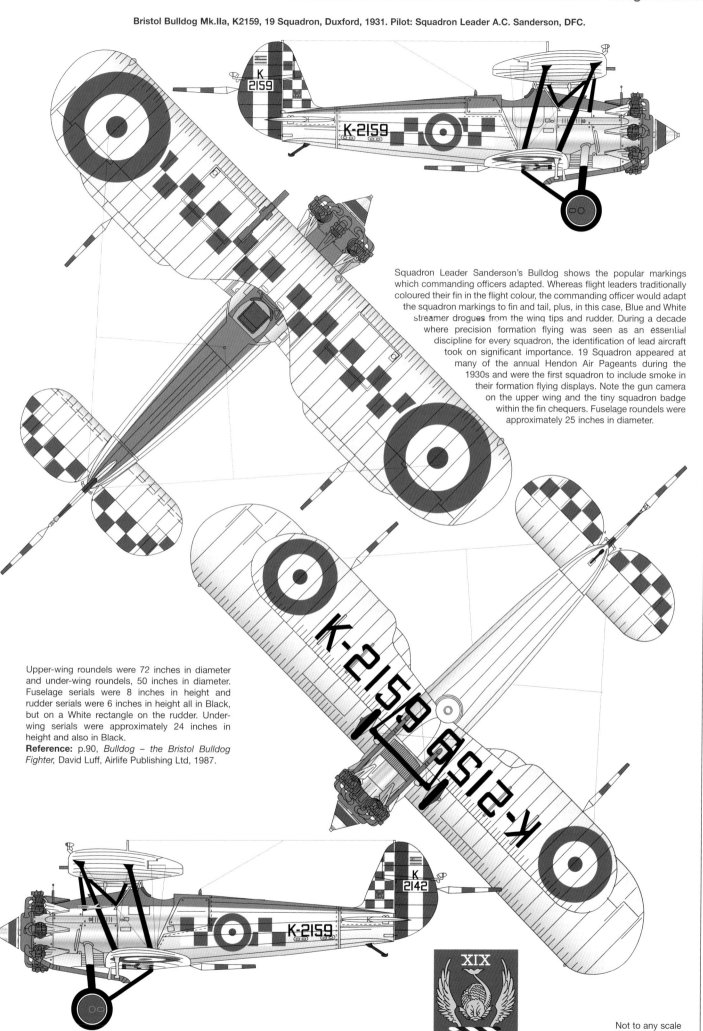

Squadron Leader Sanderson's Bulldog shows the popular markings which commanding officers adapted. Whereas flight leaders traditionally coloured their fin in the flight colour, the commanding officer would adapt the squadron markings to fin and tail, plus, in this case, Blue and White streamer drogues from the wing tips and rudder. During a decade where precision formation flying was seen as an essential discipline for every squadron, the identification of lead aircraft took on significant importance. 19 Squadron appeared at many of the annual Hendon Air Pageants during the 1930s and were the first squadron to include smoke in their formation flying displays. Note the gun camera on the upper wing and the tiny squadron badge within the fin chequers. Fuselage roundels were approximately 25 inches in diameter.

Upper-wing roundels were 72 inches in diameter and under-wing roundels, 50 inches in diameter. Fuselage serials were 8 inches in height and rudder serials were 6 inches in height all in Black, but on a White rectangle on the rudder. Under-wing serials were approximately 24 inches in height and also in Black.
Reference: p.90, *Bulldog – the Bristol Bulldog Fighter,* David Luff, Airlife Publishing Ltd, 1987.

Not to any scale

Bristol Bulldog Mk.IIa, K2142, 17 Squadron, Upavon, 1930. Squadron leader's aircraft.

By 1930, Upavon was fully equipped with Bulldogs for both 3 and 17 Squadrons. Later, in 1934, both squadrons were moved to Kenley as their new base. 17 Squadron's distinctive zigzag markings came in many shapes and sizes. K2142 displays an abbreviated version of the marking, while earlier aircraft carried the zigzag the full length of the fuselage. As a commanding officer's aircraft, K2142 carried the Black fin with commander's emblem. Fuselage roundels were approximately 25 inches in diameter. Upper-wing roundels were 72 inches in diameter and under-wing roundels, 50 inches in diameter. Fuselage serials were 8 inches in height and rudder serials were 6 inches in height all in Black, but on a White rectangle on the rudder. Under-wing serials were approximately 24 inches in height and also in Black.

Reference: p.130, *On Silver Wings*, Alec Lumsden and Owen Thetford, Osprey Aerospace, 1993.

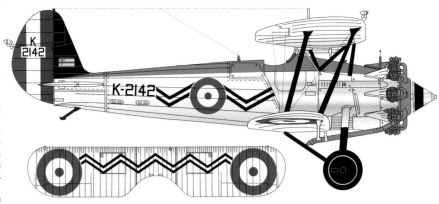

Bristol Bulldog Mk.IIa, K2184, 41 Squadron, Northolt, 1931.

41 Squadron Bulldogs were one of the few units not to use the anti-glare treatment on their top decking. K2184 proudly displays the squadron badge on its fin – the Cross of Lorraine surmounted by a crown. Also note the aircraft's individual identification letter on the nose and no Silver outline to the fuselage serials. Fuselage roundels were approximately 25 inches in diameter. Upper-wing roundels were 72 inches in diameter and under-wing roundels, 50 inches in diameter. Fuselage serials were 8 inches in height and rudder serials were 6 inches in height all in Black, but on a White rectangle on the rudder. Under-wing serials were approximately 24 inches in height and also in Black.

Reference: p.295, *Aircraft in Detail – the Bristol Bulldog*, Sue J. Bushell, Scale Aircraft Modelling, April 1992.

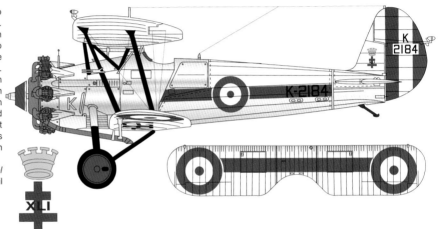

Bristol Bulldog Mk.IIa, K2210, 29 Squadron, North Weald, 1932.

29 Squadron was another squadron which found the need to drastically reduce the fuselage markings to just two of its famous 'X's. K2210 was a 'A' Flight leader's aircraft and as such displayed the traditional Red fin. The Bristol factory's bulldog logo was retained on the fin. Fuselage roundels were approximately 25 inches in diameter. Upper-wing roundels were 72 inches in diameter and under-wing roundels, 50 inches in diameter. Fuselage serials were 8 inches in height and rudder serials were 6 inches in height all in Black, but on a White rectangle on the rudder. Under-wing serials were approximately 24 inches in height and also in Black.

Reference: p.337, *Bristol Bulldog II, IIa: Part 1*, Richard Ward, Aircraft Modelworld, December 1984.

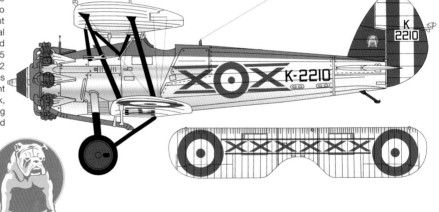

Not to any scale

Bristol Bulldog Mk.IIa, K1641, 54 Squadron, Hornchurch, 1934.

K1641 displayed the Yellow bar squadron marking in its abbreviated form. On earlier aircraft, the bar was extended both sides of the roundel. In 1936, the squadron was given permission to change its markings to a Red band with Silver diagonals (similar to 32 Squadron). Note the absence of anti-glare paint on the top decking. Fuselage roundels were approximately 25 inches in diameter. Upper-wing roundels were 72 inches in diameter and under-wing roundels, 50 inches in diameter. Fuselage serials were 8 inches in height and rudder serials were 6 inches in height all in Black. The fuselage serials were outlined in Silver and the rudder serials were mounted on a White rectangle. Under-wing serials were approximately 24 inches in height and also in Black.

Reference: p.337, *Bristol Bulldog II, IIa: Part 1*, Richard Ward, Aircraft Modelworld, December 1984.

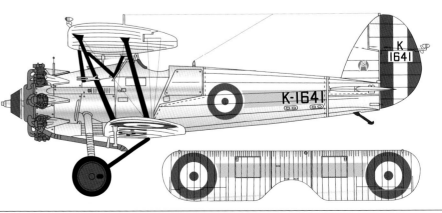

Bristol Bulldog Mk.IIa, K1676, 23 Squadron, Kenley, 14 December 1931. Pilot: Pilot Officer Douglas R.S. Bader.

Pilot Officer Bader had been a commissioned officer in the Royal Air Force for eighteen months and had already shown an aptitude for aerobatics flying, being selected to fly in a Gamecock display at Hendon earlier that year. On Monday 14 December 1931, Douglas Bader flew from Kenley to Woodley airfield along with two other pilots from his squadron. In the Woodley clubhouse, while discussing aerobatics, Bader was asked to give a demonstration of low flying. Bader refused, recognising the few hours he had accumulated in Bulldogs. As Bader and the other pilots were leaving, someone dared him to do it. Bader took off, and then, on impulse, turned back toward the field. Flying low and fast across the field, he began a slow roll, but in his inexperience with the Bulldog, he flew too low. The Bulldog's left wing struck the ground, and the plane cart-wheeled quickly into a tangle of wreckage. Thus began an incredible story of a remarkable man who would become a legend in his own lifetime. Fuselage roundels were approximately 25 inches in diameter.

23
SEMPER AGRESSUS

Upper-wing roundels were 72 inches in diameter and under-wing roundels, 50 inches in diameter. Fuselage serials were 8 inches in height and rudder serials were 6 inches in height all in Black, but on a Silver rectangle on the fuselage and White rectangle on the rudder. Under-wing serials were approximately 24 inches in height and also in Black.
Reference: Artist's impression based on other 23 Squadron aircraft.

Not to any scale

Bristol Bulldog Mk.IIa, K2206, 56 Squadron, North Weald, 1932.

Three Bulldogs were experimentally fitted with short-chord polygonal cowling rings. Two were with 56 Squadron, K2206 and K2227, the third being with 111 Squadron, K1627. However, the modification was never standardised or put into production. K2206 was also retro-fitted with a wider under-carriage, Bendix brakes and a tail wheel. Note the abbreviated squadron markings on the fuselage and gap in the top wing chequered band. K2206 also carried an individual aircraft identification letter in Light Blue outlined in Black, forward of the cockpit. Fuselage roundels were approximately 25 inches in diameter. Upper-wing roundels were 72 inches in diameter and under-wing roundels, 50 inches in diameter. Fuselage serials were 8 inches in height and rudder serials were 6 inches in height all in Black, but on a White rectangle on the rudder. Under-wing serials were approximately 24 inches in height and also in Black.

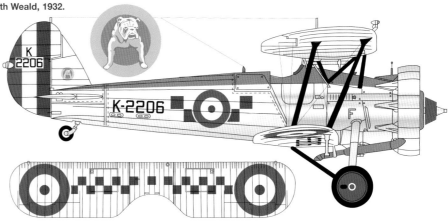

Reference: p.134, *On Silver Wings*, Alec Lumsden and Owen Thetford, Osprey Aerospace, 1993.

Bristol Bulldog Mk.IIa, K1619/1690, 32 Squadron, Biggin Hill, 1932.

32 Squadron was the third squadron to receive Bulldogs in October 1930. The true identity of K1619/1690 is unknown. Photographic reference shows this aircraft leading a flight of 32 Squadron Bulldogs while wearing the two serials. The original serial may well be K1619 with the replacement rudder from K1690 yet to be re-painted!. Note also that this aircraft was retro-fitted with new undercarriage, brakes and tail wheel. Fuselage roundels were approximately 25 inches in diameter. Upper-wing roundels were 72 inches in diameter and under-wing roundels, 50 inches in diameter. Fuselage serials were 8 inches in height and rudder serials were 6 inches in height all in Black. The fuselage serials were outlined in Silver and the rudder serials placed on a White rectangle. Under-wing serials were approximately 24 inches in height and also in Black.

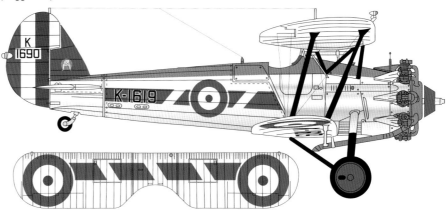

Reference: p.96, *Bulldog – the Bristol Bulldog Fighter*, David Luff, Airlife Publishing Ltd, 1987.

Bristol Bulldog TM, K3181, 19 Squadron, Duxford, 1933.

Delivery of the two-seat Bulldog TM (Training Machine) began in late 1932. A large proportion of the fifty-nine produced went to the Central Flying School, Nos.1, 3, and 5 Flying Training Schools and the RAF College at Cranwell. However, six front-line squadrons also received at least one version of the TM. K3181 was assigned to 19 Squadron. The main differences besides the two seats were a wider wheelbase, lighter engine, more angular and larger rudder and three and a half degree sweep-back on the wings. Fuselage roundels were approximately 25 inches in diameter. Upper-wing roundels were 72 inches in diameter and under-wing roundels, 50 inches in diameter. Fuselage serials were 8 inches in height and rudder serials were 6 inches in height all in Black, but on a White rectangle on the rudder. Under-wing serials were approximately 24 inches in height and also in Black.

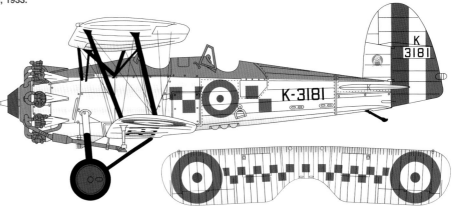

Reference: p.137, *On Silver Wings*, Alec Lumsden and Owen Thetford, Osprey Aerospace, 1993.

Bristol Bulldog TM, K3925, RAF College, Cranwell, 1934.

The RAF College at Cranwell had seven Bulldog TMs on strength. Each was given an identification number which was painted in Light Blue outlined in Black and positioned forward of the fuselage roundel. Note the absence of wheel covers and anti-glare paint on the upper decking. Fuselage roundels were approximately 25 inches in diameter. Upper-wing roundels were 72 inches in diameter and under-wing roundels, 50 inches in diameter. Fuselage serials were 8 inches in height and rudder serials were 6 inches in height all in Black, but on a White rectangle on the rudder. Under-wing serials were approximately 25 inches in height and also in Black.

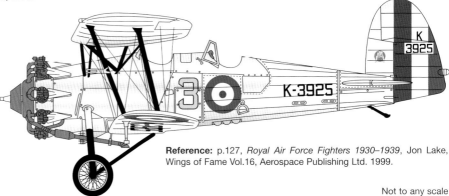

Reference: p.127, *Royal Air Force Fighters 1930–1939*, Jon Lake, Wings of Fame Vol.16, Aerospace Publishing Ltd. 1999.

Not to any scale

Bristol Bulldog Mk.II, K1081, 17 Squadron, Upavon, 1930.

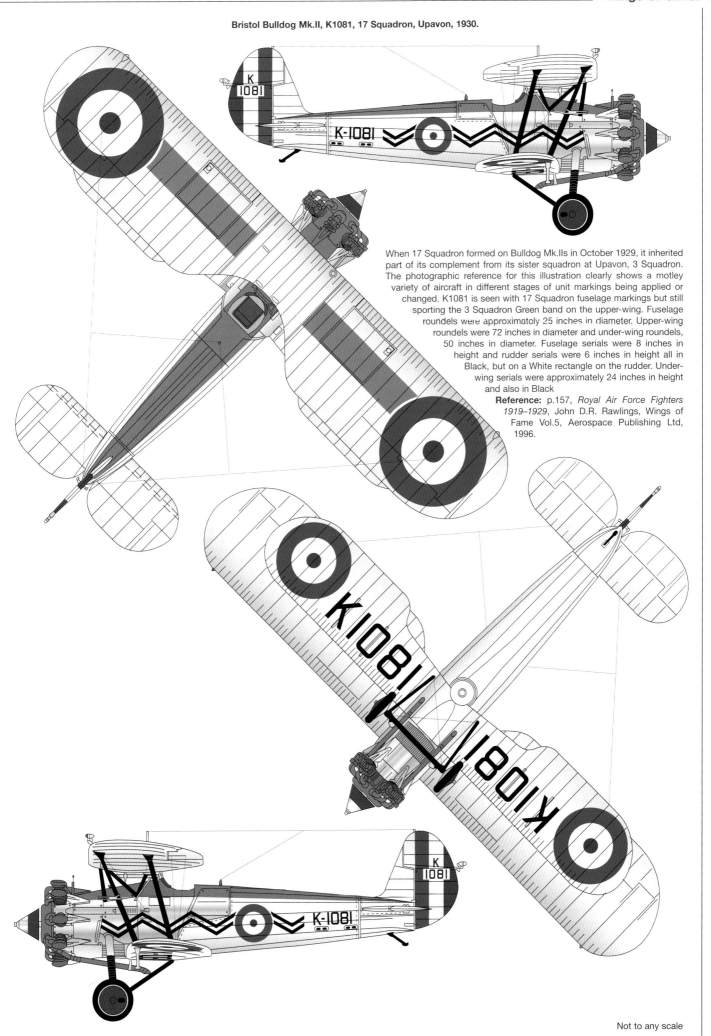

When 17 Squadron formed on Bulldog Mk.IIs in October 1929, it inherited part of its complement from its sister squadron at Upavon, 3 Squadron. The photographic reference for this illustration clearly shows a motley variety of aircraft in different stages of unit markings being applied or changed. K1081 is seen with 17 Squadron fuselage markings but still sporting the 3 Squadron Green band on the upper-wing. Fuselage roundels were approximately 25 inches in diameter. Upper-wing roundels were 72 inches in diameter and under-wing roundels, 50 inches in diameter. Fuselage serials were 8 inches in height and rudder serials were 6 inches in height all in Black, but on a White rectangle on the rudder. Under-wing serials were approximately 24 inches in height and also in Black

Reference: p.157, *Royal Air Force Fighters 1919–1929*, John D.R. Rawlings, Wings of Fame Vol.5, Aerospace Publishing Ltd, 1996.

Not to any scale

Westland Wapiti IIA, J.9719, 60 Squadron, Kohat, North-west Frontier, India, 1932.

The tribesmen of the North-west Frontier continued to be a thorn in the side of the British Army in India and 60 Squadron spent much of its operational duties assisting ground forces in trying to quell the various uprisings in this region. 60 Squadron remained based at Kohat for nine years. Its easily identifiable Black stripe marking was nicknamed the 'Kohat stripe'. The individual aircraft identification letter was positioned in a Black square aft of the fuselage roundel. Fuselage roundels were approximately 25 inches in diameter and wing roundels were 60 inches in diameter. Serials were in Black (outlined in White on the rudder) and were 8 inches in height. Under-wing serials were also in Black and approximately 30 inches in height.
Reference: p.34, *Wapiti and Wallace,* Owen Thetford, Aeroplane Monthly, October, 1994.

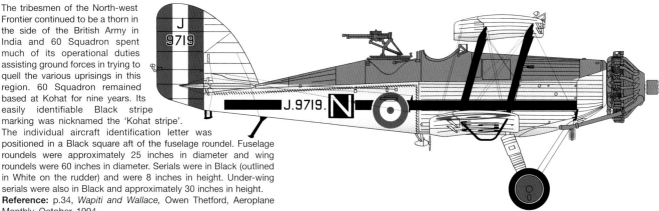

Westland Wapiti IIA, J.9632, 'C' Flight, 55 Squadron, Hinaidi, Iraq, 1932.

55 Squadron aircraft carried the flight letter and individual aircraft number on the nose. The squadron badge was displayed on the fin. Of interest on J.9632 were the White dashes along the fuselage, just inside the demarcation of the Dark Green anti-glare paint. This may have been as a visual aid for rescue purposes, should the aircraft force-land in desert conditions. Also of note was the removal of the wheel covers. This was often the practice when aircraft had to use rough and muddy landing strips. Fuselage roundels were approximately 25 inches in diameter and wing roundels were 60 inches in diameter. Serials were in Black (outlined in White on the rudder) and were 8 inches in height. Under-wing serials were also in Black and approximately 30 inches in height.
Reference: http://www.raf.mod.uk/downloads/gallery/h1221.jpg

Westland Wapiti IIA, K-1309, 5 Squadron, Risalpur, India, 1938. Pilot: Flying Officer Emerton.

K-1309 carried the squadron marking of a broad Black band around the fuselage aft of the roundel and the squadron badge of a Maple Leaf within the Army Co-operation symbol of a White five-pointed star. Also noticeable on this aircraft was the attachment of a long hook. This was the standard method for retrieving messages from ground troops. Fuselage roundels were approximately 25 inches in diameter and wing roundels were approximately 40 inches in diameter. Serials were in Black and were 8 inches in height. Under-wing serials were also in Black and approximately 30 inches in height.
Reference: p.19, *Wapiti and Wallace,* Owen Thetford, Aeroplane Monthly, August 1994.

Westland Wapiti IIA, K-1291, 27 Squadron, Kohat, India, 1938. Squadron Commander's aircraft.

K-1291 was flown by each succeeding squadron commander of 27 Squadron. The squadron marking was a Red fuselage band next to the tail and the famous Green elephant badge on the fin. On this occasion the elephant was within the 'Grenade' symbol used to identify bomber units. Fuselage roundels were approximately 25 inches in diameter and wing roundels were approximately 40 inches in diameter. Serials were in Black and were 8 inches in height (note the White or Silver outline to the serials overlapping the fuselage band). Under-wing serials were also in Black and approximately 30 inches in height.
Reference: p.226, *RAF Operations 1918–1938,* Chaz Bowyer, William Kimber & Co. Ltd. 1988.

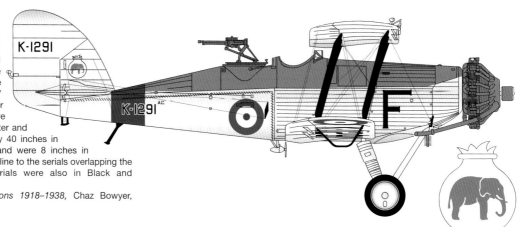

Not to any scale

Westland Wapiti IIA, J.9408, 'A' Flight, 30 Squadron, Mosul, Iraq, August 1932.

During this period, 30 Squadron participated in quelling rebellious tribesmen by supporting ground forces. Of note was Sheikh Mahmud's surrender in 1931 and operations against Sheikh Ahmad of Barzan on the northern borders with Turkey in 1932. J.9408 followed the customary practice of 30 Squadron of painting its aircraft's wingtips as a recognition aid for emergency landings. The squadron badge of a palm tree centred on the squadron number was painted on the rear fuselage (subsequently moved to the fin) and the flight letter in 'Arabic' style was painted on the nose. Note also the fatter tyres on this aircraft. Fuselage roundels were approximately 25 inches in diameter and wing roundels were 60 inches in diameter. Serials were in Black (outlined in White on the rudder) and were 8 inches in height.

Reference: p.18, *Wapiti and Wallace,* Owen Thetford, Aeroplane Monthly, September, 1994.

Not to any scale

Westland Wapiti IIA, J.9835, 'C' Flight, 84 Squadron, Shaibah, Iraq, 1931.

The White triangle outlined in Black, was used as the flight symbol for 'C' Flight of 84 Squadron. As well as on the fin, it also appeared under the lower wings and centrally, on top of the upper-wing. The flight symbol was also repeated on the wheel covers. J.9835 carried the squadron badge of a scorpion and the squadron number on the nose. Fuselage roundels were approximately 25 inches in diameter and wing roundels were 60 inches in diameter. Serials were in Black (outlined in White on the rudder) and were 8 inches in height.
Reference: p.97 *RAF Operations 1918–1938* by Chaz Bowyer, William Kimber & Co. Ltd. 1988.

Westland Wapiti IIA, K.2237, 605 (County of Warwick) Squadron, Castle Bromwich, 1932.

605 Squadron markings consisted of the squadron number appearing large and forward of the fuselage roundel. To the rear of the fuselage roundel appeared the squadron badge which incorporated the County of Warwick coat of arms along with the RAF eagle. The Auxiliary Squadron Wapitis became regular top-billing at the Hendon Air Shows during the early 1930s, demonstrating formation flying together with fighter aircraft. Fuselage roundels were approximately 25 inches in diameter and wing roundels were 60 inches in diameter. Serials were in Black (outlined in White on the rudder) and were 8 inches in height. Under-wing serials were also in Black and approximately 30 inches in height.
Reference: p.35, *Wapiti and Wallace,* Owen Thetford, Aeroplane Monthly, October 1994.

Westland Wapiti IIA, K-1339, 600 (City of London) Squadron, Hendon, 1933. 'A' Flight leader's aircraft.

The Wapiti appeared in the United Kingdom much later than it did overseas. Even then it was only allocated to the Auxiliary Squadrons. 600 Squadron was the second squadron to receive Wapitis, which they operated between 1929 and 1935. The squadron markings were the large squadron number appearing aft of the fuselage roundel and the coat of arms of the City of London on the fin. Fuselage roundels were approximately 25 inches in diameter and wing roundels were 60 inches in diameter. Serials were in Black (outlined in White on the rudder) and were 8 inches in height. Under-wing serials were also in Black and approximately 30 inches in height.
Reference: p.21 *Wapiti and Wallace* by Owen Thetford, Aeroplane Monthly, September 1994.

Westland Wapiti IIA, J-9388, 31 Squadron, Karachi (Drigh Road), India, 1936.

Two fuselage bands in flight colours, aft of the roundel, were the squadron markings for 31 Squadron. The squadron badge of a five-pointed star within a wreath was displayed on the fin. This was shown within the six-pointed star symbol identifying the squadron as an Army Co-operation unit. Fuselage roundels were approximately 25 inches in diameter and wing roundels were approximately 40 inches in diameter. Serials were in Black and were 8 inches in height (note the Silver cut-out where serial over-laps the rear fuselage band). Under-wing serials were also in Black and approximately 30 inches in height.
Reference: p.71, *Aircraft Camouflage and Markings 1907–1954*, Bruce Robertson, Harleyford Publications Limited, 1956.

Not to any scale

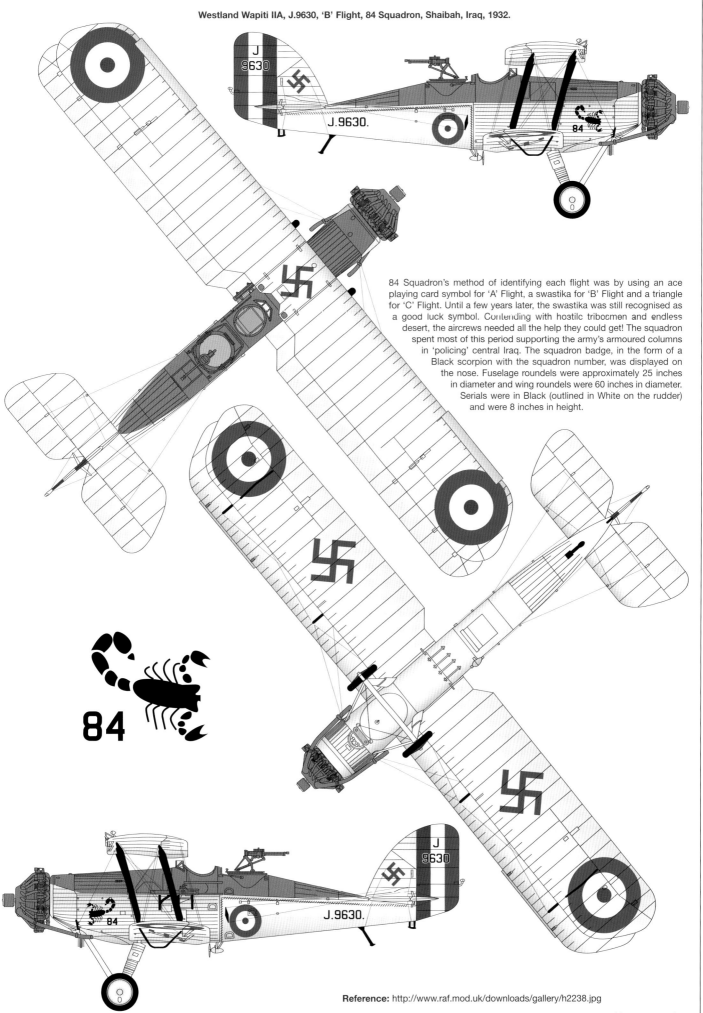

Westland Wapiti IIA, J.9630, 'B' Flight, 84 Squadron, Shaibah, Iraq, 1932.

84 Squadron's method of identifying each flight was by using an ace playing card symbol for 'A' Flight, a swastika for 'B' Flight and a triangle for 'C' Flight. Until a few years later, the swastika was still recognised as a good luck symbol. Contending with hostile tribesmen and endless desert, the aircrews needed all the help they could get! The squadron spent most of this period supporting the army's armoured columns in 'policing' central Iraq. The squadron badge, in the form of a Black scorpion with the squadron number, was displayed on the nose. Fuselage roundels were approximately 25 inches in diameter and wing roundels were 60 inches in diameter. Serials were in Black (outlined in White on the rudder) and were 8 inches in height.

Reference: http://www.raf.mod.uk/downloads/gallery/h2238.jpg

Not to any scale

Avro Tutor, K.3225, Cambridge University Air Squadron, Duxford, 1933.

The Avro Tutor became standard equipment for all University Air Squadrons up until 1939. The Munich Crisis and the following period of re-armament, required a massive increase in the number of pilot and officer recruits, and many more University Air Squadrons were formed before and during the war years to provide for this need. The UAS acted as another type of training unit for the RAF. Not only were the trainees volunteers, but also well educated. K.3225 was the squadron commander's aircraft as shown by the fin badge. The only other marking being the squadron badge, which was displayed below the cockpit. Other Tutors would wear the Cambridge colours of Red, Dark Blue and Light Blue as a fuselage stripe. Fuselage roundels were approximately 25 inches in diameter. Upper- and lower-wing roundels were approximately 40 inches in diameter. Fuselage and rudder serials were painted in Black (with White outlines on the rudder) and were 8 inches in height.

Reference: p.78, *An Illustrated History of the RAF*, Roy Conyers Nesbit, Coombe Books, 1990.

Avro Tutor, K.3296, 3 Flying Training School, Grantham, 1933.

3 FTS aircraft carried a simple fuselage band as their flight marking. This may have been in the appropriate flight colour for each aircraft. The individual aircraft identification letter was positioned aft of the fuselage roundel and was in Red. Fuselage roundels were approximately 25 inches in diameter. Upper- and lower-wing roundels were approximately 40 inches in diameter. Fuselage and rudder serials were painted in Black (with White outlines on the rudder) and were 8 inches in height.
Reference: www.rafmuseum.org 'Milestones of Flight'

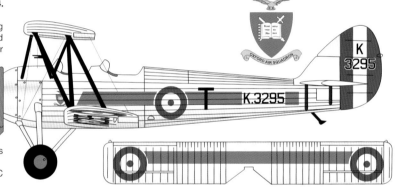

Avro Tutor, K.3295, Oxford University Air Squadron, Duxford, 1934.

The Oxford University Air Squadron was another popular flying training unit among the young educated men of the 1930s. Many distinguished pilots and commanders of Second World War squadrons, started their career with such units. K.3295 carried the well-known 'Oxford Blue' markings both as a fuselage band and spanning the upper wing. The Oxford UAS badge was positioned below the front cockpit. The individual aircraft identification letter, 'T' was in Black and positioned aft of the fuselage roundel. Fuselage roundels were approximately 25 inches in diameter. Upper- and lower-wing roundels were approximately 40 inches in diameter. Fuselage and rudder serials were painted in Black (with White outlines on the rudder) and were 8 inches in height.
Reference: p.409, *RAF Pilots in Training*, Major Oliver Stewart, MC AFC, War in the Air, Part 13, The Amalgamated Press Ltd. 1936

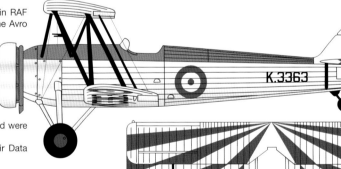

Avro Tutor, K.3363, Central Flying School, Wittering, 1935.

One of the main roles of the Central Flying School was to train RAF flying instructors. Having some of the best pilots in the RAF, the Avro Tutors of the CFS were well known for their aerobatics displays during the mid-1930s. The Red and White sunburst design on the wings and tail planes may well have originated as a recognition marking for their public displays. K.3363 also had Dark Green (possibly Nivo) applied to its upper fuselage decking. Fuselage roundels were approximately 25 inches in diameter. Upper- and lower-wing roundels were approximately 35 inches in diameter. Fuselage and rudder serials were painted in Black and were 8 inches in height.
Reference: p.19, *Spitfire: a Test Pilot's Story*, Jeffrey Quill, Air Data Publications, 1996

Avro Tutor, K.3215, RAF College, Cranwell, 1936.

The RAF took over responsibility of Cranwell when the RNAS and Royal Flying Corps were amalgamated in 1918. Instigated by Sir Hugh Trenchard, it became the RAF College in February 1920, tasked with training a dedicated officer corps for the RAF. One of its most famous cadets was Sir Frank Whittle who gained his commission at Cranwell in 1928. Part of his final thesis while at Cranwell contained his early ideas on jet propulsion. K.3215 depicts the all-over trainer Yellow and polished metal panels adopted by the RAF for its trainers during the late 1930s. The RAF College badge was displayed on the fin. Fuselage roundels were approximately 25 inches in diameter. Upper- and lower-wing roundels were approximately 35 inches in diameter. Fuselage and rudder serials were painted in Black and were 8 inches in height.
Reference: www.shuttleworth.org

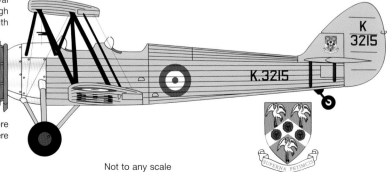

Not to any scale

Hawker Hart (India), K2091, 11 Squadron, Risalpur, India, 1937.

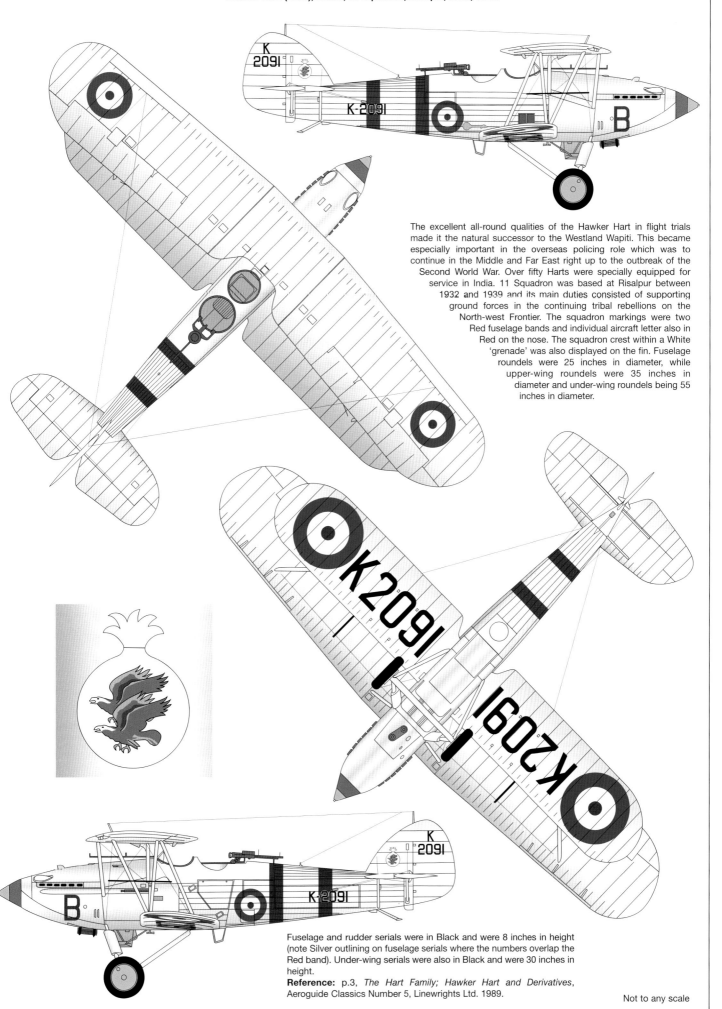

The excellent all-round qualities of the Hawker Hart in flight trials made it the natural successor to the Westland Wapiti. This became especially important in the overseas policing role which was to continue in the Middle and Far East right up to the outbreak of the Second World War. Over fifty Harts were specially equipped for service in India. 11 Squadron was based at Risalpur between 1932 and 1939 and its main duties consisted of supporting ground forces in the continuing tribal rebellions on the North-west Frontier. The squadron markings were two Red fuselage bands and individual aircraft letter also in Red on the nose. The squadron crest within a White 'grenade' was also displayed on the fin. Fuselage roundels were 25 inches in diameter, while upper-wing roundels were 35 inches in diameter and under-wing roundels being 55 inches in diameter.

Fuselage and rudder serials were in Black and were 8 inches in height (note Silver outlining on fuselage serials where the numbers overlap the Red band). Under-wing serials were also in Black and were 30 inches in height.

Reference: p.3, *The Hart Family; Hawker Hart and Derivatives*, Aeroguide Classics Number 5, Linewrights Ltd. 1989.

Not to any scale

Hawker Hart SEDB, K1430, 33 Squadron, Bicester, 1933.

33 Squadron was the first to equip with Hawker Harts in 1930. To signify this, the squadron adopted the Hart badge as its insignia. The SEDB suffix stands for 'Single-Engine Day Bomber'. 33 Squadron also took the unusual step of positioning their squadron number above the fuselage roundel. Fuselage roundels were 25 inches in diameter. Upper-wing roundels were 65 inches in diameter and under-wing roundels were 55 inches in diameter. Fuselage and rudder serials were 8 inches in height (outlined in White on the rudder). Under-wing serials were also Black and were 30 inches in height.
Reference: p.191, *The Hawker Hart Family*, Sue J. Bushell, Scale Aircraft Modelling, February 1993.

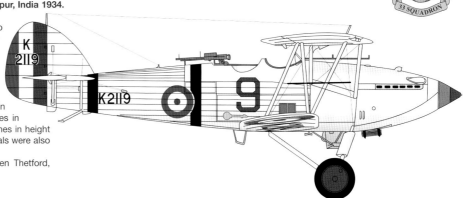

Hawker Hart (India) ,K2119, 39 Squadron, Risalpur, India 1934.

39 Squadron flew over 'the Grim' from 1931 to 1939. This was the traditional name given by the British Army in India for the troublesome North-west Frontier. The Hawker Hart became the ideal replacement for the ageing Wapitis and took up all the policing roles, which their predecessors carried out. Fuselage roundels were 25 inches in diameter. Upper-wing roundels were 65 inches in diameter and under-wing roundels were 55 inches in diameter. Fuselage and rudder serials were 8 inches in height (outlined in White on the rudder). Under-wing serials were also Black and were 30 inches in height.
Reference: p.52, *Hawker Harts and Hinds*, Owen Thetford, Aeroplane Monthly, July 1995.

Hawker Hart SEDB, K3900, 57 Squadron, Upper Heyford, 1934.

57 Squadron displayed their squadron number in the appropriate flight colour forward of the fuselage roundel. As well as its day-bomber role, aircraft from 57 Squadron were also used to test the aircraft's dive-bombing capabilities. Fuselage roundels were 25 inches in diameter. Upper-wing roundels were 65 inches in diameter and under-wing roundels were 55 inches in diameter. Fuselage and rudder serials were 8 inches in height (outlined in White on the rudder). Under-wing serials were also Black and were 30 inches in height.
Reference: p.13, *Hawker Harts and Hinds,* Owen Thetford, Aeroplane Monthly, May 1995.

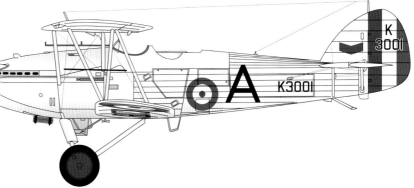

Hawker Hart (C), K3001, 24 Squadron, Kenley, 1934.

24 Squadron's prime role at this time was as an air transport and communications unit. It was used to fly many important VIPs, including members of the Royal family. The squadron insignia of a Red chevron was displayed on the fin and a large aircraft identification letter was painted on the fuselage on a White background. Fuselage roundels were 25 inches in diameter. Upper-wing roundels were 65 inches in diameter and under-wing roundels were 55 inches in diameter. Fuselage and rudder serials were 8 inches in height (outlined in White on the rudder). Under-wing serials were also Black and were 30 inches in height.
Reference: p.51 *Hawker Harts and Hinds* by Owen Thetford, Aeroplane Monthly, July 1995.

Hawker Hart SEDB, K3900, 15 Squadron, Abingdon, 1935.

15 Squadron took the unusual step of displaying their squadron number in Roman numerals. The squadron leader's pennant also carried the 'XV' between the two lower bars. Fuselage roundels were 25 inches in diameter. Upper-wing roundels were 35 inches in diameter and under-wing roundels were 55 inches in diameter. Fuselage and rudder serials were 8 inches in height. Under-wing serials were also Black and were 30 inches in height.
Reference: p.55, *Hawker Harts and Hinds,* Owen Thetford, Aeroplane Monthly, July 1995.

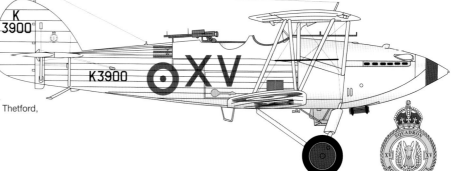

Not to any scale

Hawker Audax, K7425, 9 Service Flying Training Squadron, Hullavington, April 1940.

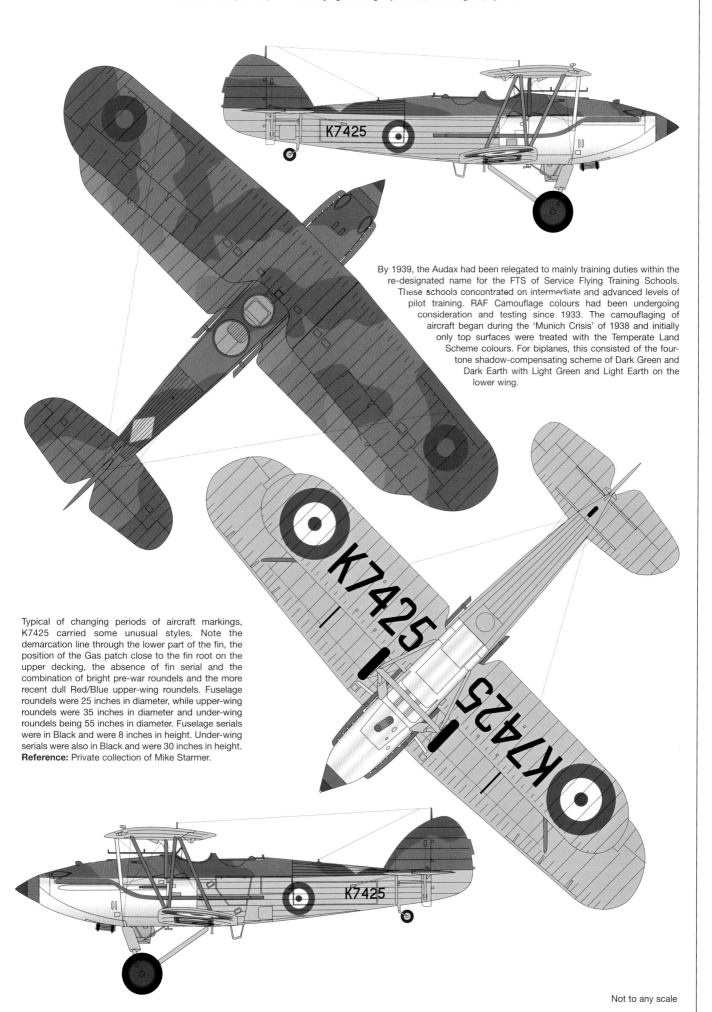

By 1939, the Audax had been relegated to mainly training duties within the re-designated name for the FTS of Service Flying Training Schools. These schools concontrated on intermediate and advanced levels of pilot training. RAF Camouflage colours had been undergoing consideration and testing since 1933. The camouflaging of aircraft began during the 'Munich Crisis' of 1938 and initially only top surfaces were treated with the Temperate Land Scheme colours. For biplanes, this consisted of the four-tone shadow-compensating scheme of Dark Green and Dark Earth with Light Green and Light Earth on the lower wing.

Typical of changing periods of aircraft markings, K7425 carried some unusual styles. Note the demarcation line through the lower part of the fin, the position of the Gas patch close to the fin root on the upper decking, the absence of fin serial and the combination of bright pre-war roundels and the more recent dull Red/Blue upper-wing roundels. Fuselage roundels were 25 inches in diameter, while upper-wing roundels were 35 inches in diameter and under-wing roundels being 55 inches in diameter. Fuselage serials were in Black and were 8 inches in height. Under-wing serials were also in Black and were 30 inches in height.
Reference: Private collection of Mike Starmer.

Not to any scale

Hawker Audax, K3056, 2 Squadron, Manston, 1934.

K3056 is shown carrying the Audax's renowned 'message hook'. This was used to pick up messages from ground forces. The Black triangle was one of 2 Squadron's flight symbols. Fuselage roundels were 25 inches in diameter. Upper-wing roundels were 65 inches in diameter and under-wing roundels were 55 inches in diameter. Fuselage and rudder serials were 8 inches in height (outlined in White on the rudder and Silver on the fuselage). Under-wing serials were also Black and were 30 inches in height.
Reference: p.194, *The Hawker Hart Family*, Sue J. Bushell, Scale Aircraft Modelling, Feburary 1993.

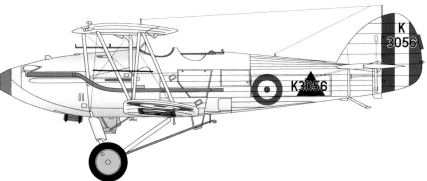

Hawker Audax, K4852, 28 Squadron, Ambala, India 1936.

The Audax quickly followed the Hart into overseas service. Built as the Army Co-operation variant, it met all of the RAF's demands in the Middle East and North-west Frontier theatres. Second only to the Hart in production figures, over 700 were produced. K4852 carried the Army Co-operation star symbol on its fin containing the squadron badge. Fuselage roundels were 25 inches in diameter. Upper-wing roundels were 35 inches in diameter and under-wing roundels were 55 inches in diameter. Fuselage and rudder serials were 8 inches in height while under-wing serials were 30 inches in height.
Reference: p.11, *The Family: Hawker Hart and Derivatives,* Aeroguide Classics No.5, Linewrights Ltd. 1989.

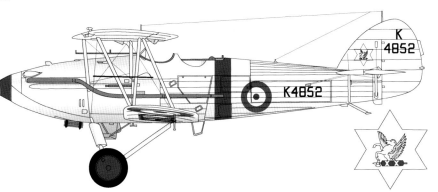

Hawker Audax, K5150, Royal Air Force College, Cranwell, 1936.

The Hawker Hart also had a distinguished career as a training aircraft and equipped many of the Flying Training Schools in the late thirties. It was used for pilot training and also observer, gunnery and bomb aiming. K5150 carried the College crest on the fin. This consists of three Storks spreading their wings to fly and three lion's heads signifying the College's Royal Charter. Fuselage roundels were 25 inches in diameter. Upper-wing roundels were 35 inches in diameter and under-wing roundels were 55 inches in diameter. Fuselage and rudder serials were 8 inches in height and under-wing serials were also Black and were 30 inches in height.
Reference: Private collection of Mike Starmer.

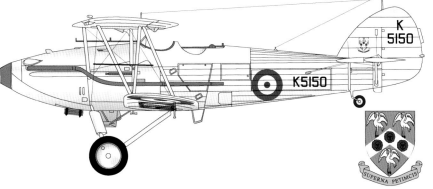

Hawker Audax, K7518, 4 Flying Training School, Abu Sueir, Egypt, 1936.

4 Flying Training School (FTS) was responsible for pilot training in the Middle East. The Harts and Audaxes at Abu Sueir saw continuous service training hundreds of pilots, observers and gunners in the lead up to the Second World War. During the war, 4 FTS continued its training role at Habbaniyah, Iraq. It was here that the Audax was finally used in anger, defending Habbaniyah against pro-Axis rebels and also German and Italian air strikes. Fuselage roundels were 25 inches in diameter. Upper-wing roundels were 35 inches in diameter and under-wing roundels were 55 inches in diameter. Fuselage and rudder serials were 8 inches in height and under-wing serials were also Black and were 30 inches in height.

Reference: p.194, *The Hawker Hart Family*, Sue J. Bushell, Scale Aircraft Modelling, Feburary 1993.

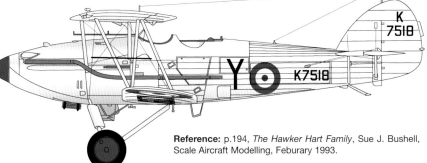

Hawker Audax, K4853, 28 Squadron, Kohat, India, 1939.

28 Squadron's Audaxes were required to soldier on in India until they were replaced by Lysanders in 1941. K4853 is shown here wearing its early pre-war squadron codes of 'BF' plus the individual aircraft letter 'J'. Fuselage roundels were 25 inches in diameter. Upper-wing roundels were 35 inches in diameter and under-wing roundels were 55 inches in diameter. Fuselage and rudder serials were 8 inches in height and under-wing serials were also Black and were 30 inches in height.
Reference: p.195, *The Hawker Hart Family*, Sue J. Bushell, Scale Aircraft Modelling, Feburary 1993.

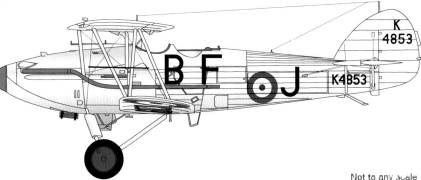

Not to any scale

Hawker Hind, K4644, 34 Squadron, Lympne, 1937.

K4644 is another example of the vagaries of positioning and style of squadron numbers that took place during this period. The colour of the numbers would relate to the particular flight which each aircraft was in. 'A' Flight – Red, 'B' Flight – Yellow and 'C' Flight – Blue. Fuselage roundels were 25 inches in diameter. Upper-wing roundels were 35 inches in diameter and under-wing roundels were 55 inches in diameter. Fuselage and rudder serials were in Black and 8 inches in height while under-wing serials were 30 inches in height.
Reference: p.42, *Hawker Hart and Hind*, Owen Thetford, Aeroplane Monthly, August 1995.

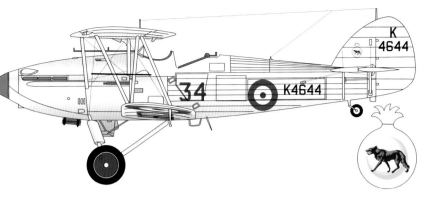

Hawker Hind, K5443, 49 Squadron, Scampton, 1938.

The Hawker Hind was taken into service by no fewer than thirty-one regular squadrons and fourteen auxiliary squadrons between 1935 and 1938. This amounted to virtually all of the RAF's bombing squadrons. It was only a marginal improvement over the Hart, but this included a higher performing engine, rams-horn exhaust ejectors and a re-designed gunner's rear cockpit. As per standard during this period, K5443 carried the minimal markings of its squadron number, in flight colour, on the fuselage and squadron badge on the fin. Fuselage roundels were 25 inches in diameter. Upper-wing roundels were 35 inches in diameter and under-wing roundels were 55 inches in diameter. Fuselage and rudder serials were in Black and 8 inches in height while under-wing serials were 30 inches in height.

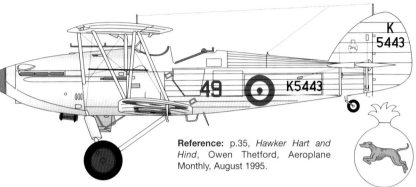

Reference: p.35, *Hawker Hart and Hind*, Owen Thetford, Aeroplane Monthly, August 1995.

Hawker Hind K6845, 609 (West Riding) Squadron, Auxiliary Air Force, Yeadon, 1938.

609 Squadron was one of the Yorkshire Riding's Auxiliary squadrons. The squadron took the unusual step of displaying their squadron number quite small and high up on the fuselage near the pilot's cockpit. The squadron's badge, a White rose and crossed hunting horns, was depicted on the fin inside the bombing squadron grenade symbol. Fuselage roundels were 25 inches in diameter. Upper-wing roundels were 35 inches in diameter and under-wing roundels were 55 inches in diameter. Fuselage and rudder serials were in Black and 8 inches in height while under-wing serials were 30 inches in height.
Reference: p39, *Hawker Hart and Hind*, Owen Thetford, Aeroplane Monthly, August 1995.

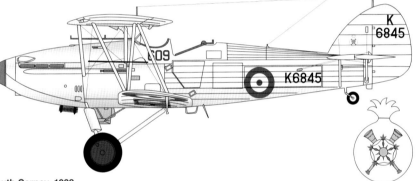

Hawker Hart Trainer, K4927, 3 Flying Training School, South Cerney, 1938.

In 1934, the realisation that Germany was set on a path of re-armament prompted the UK government into establishing its Air Expansion programme. This increased the Home Defence squadrons from 53 to 123 by 1937 and its five Flying Training Schools were increased to eleven to meet the demand for more pilots and personnel. K4927 is depicted with its blind flying hood closed. Fuselage roundels were 25 inches in diameter. Upper-wing roundels were 35 inches in diameter and under-wing roundels were 55 inches in diameter. Fuselage and rudder serials were in Black and 8 inches in height while under-wing serials were 30 inches in height.
Reference: p.427, *RAF Piston Trainers No.11 – Hawker Hart Trainer*, Kenneth E Wixey, Aeroplane Monthly, August 1981.

Hawker Hart Trainer, K5894, 3 Flying Training School, South Cerney, 1940.

By 1940, trainer aircraft colours and markings had more or less become standardised. The Trainer Yellow on K5894 covered all of the fuselage and lower surfaces apart from the polished metal engine cowling panels. Upper surfaces were painted in the Temperate Land Scheme using the four-tone shadow compensating scheme, Dark Green and Dark Earth and Light Green and Light Earth. The upper-wing tips were also painted Trainer Yellow. Noticeable about this aircraft was the retention of pre-war roundels and White serials on the camouflaged fin. Fuselage roundels were 25 inches in diameter. Upper-wing roundels were 35 inches in diameter and under-wing roundels were 55 inches in diameter. Fuselage and rudder serials were 8 inches in height while under-wing serials were 30 inches in height.

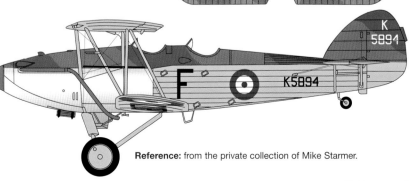

Reference: from the private collection of Mike Starmer.

Not to any scale

Hawker Demon, K4520, 64 Squadron, Martlesham Heath, June 1937.

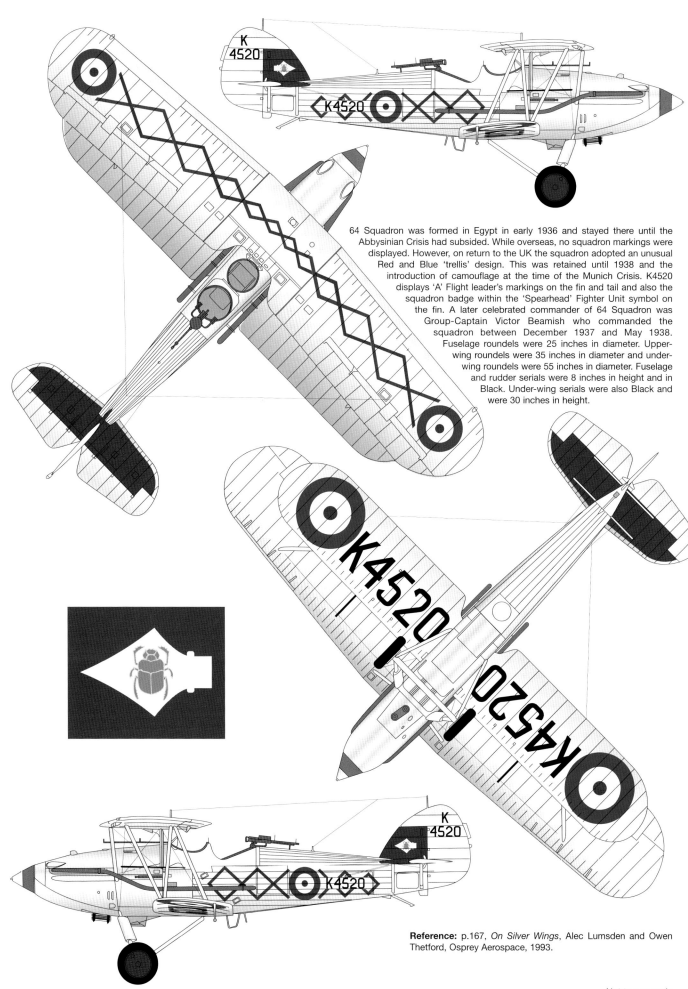

64 Squadron was formed in Egypt in early 1936 and stayed there until the Abbysinian Crisis had subsided. While overseas, no squadron markings were displayed. However, on return to the UK the squadron adopted an unusual Red and Blue 'trellis' design. This was retained until 1938 and the introduction of camouflage at the time of the Munich Crisis. K4520 displays 'A' Flight leader's markings on the fin and tail and also the squadron badge within the 'Spearhead' Fighter Unit symbol on the fin. A later celebrated commander of 64 Squadron was Group-Captain Victor Beamish who commanded the squadron between December 1937 and May 1938. Fuselage roundels were 25 inches in diameter. Upper-wing roundels were 35 inches in diameter and under-wing roundels were 55 inches in diameter. Fuselage and rudder serials were 8 inches in height and in Black. Under-wing serials were also Black and were 30 inches in height.

Reference: p.167, *On Silver Wings*, Alec Lumsden and Owen Thetford, Osprey Aerospace, 1993.

Not to any scale

Hawker Hart Fighter, K1955, 23 Squadron, Biggin Hill, 1934.

The Hart Fighter, later to be renamed the Demon, originated in 1930 as an interceptor capable of catching the new Hart bombers. This was made possible by up-rating the Kestrel engine and providing it with two forward-firing machine guns. 23 Squadron received the first batch of Hart Fighters in 1931, flying one flight of Harts with its two other flights of Bulldogs. Fuselage roundels were 25 inches in diameter. Upper-wing roundels were 65 inches in diameter and under-wing roundels were 55 inches in diameter. Fuselage and rudder serials were 8 inches in height and in Black (outlined in White on the rudder). Under-wing serials were also Black and were 30 inches in height.

Reference: p.166, *On Silver Wings*, Alec Lumsden and Owen Thetford, Osprey Aerospace, 1993.

Hawker Hart, K2966, 601 (County of London) Squadron, Auxiliary Air Force, Hendon, 1934.

The London Auxiliary Air Force Squadrons (Nos. 600, 601 and 604), based at Hendon were temporarily provided with Hawker Harts but tasked with the role of fighters. They too adopted the colourful markings of fighter units, 601 Squadron opting for a band of Red and Black inter-locking triangles in a band along the fuselage and across the top wing. The squadron badge, a Red winged sword, was also displayed on the fin. Fuselage roundels were 25 inches in diameter. Upper-wing roundels were 65 inches in diameter and under-wing roundels were 55 inches in diameter. Fuselage and rudder serials were 8 inches in height and in Black (outlined in White on the rudder). Under-wing serials were also Black and were 30 inches in height.

Reference: p.254, *Pre-War Royal Air Force Fighters*, Ray Sturtivant, Scale Aircraft Modelling, March 1983.

Hawker Demon, K3974, 29 Squadron, North Weald, July 1935.

In late 1935, 29 Squadron along with 41 Squadron, were sent to the Middle East to defend British interests there during the Abbysinian Crisis. However, engine problems caused by the ingestion of sand, resulted in the squadron temporarily re-equipping with Fairey Gordons. Fuselage roundels were 25 inches in diameter. Upper-wing roundels were 35 inches in diameter and under-wing roundels were 55 inches in diameter. Fuselage and rudder serials were 8 inches in height and in Black. Under-wing serials were also Black and were 30 inches in height.
Reference: p.164, *On Silver Wings*, Alec Lumsden and Owen Thetford, Osprey Aerospace, 1993.

Hawker Hart, K2986, 600 (City of London) Squadron, Auxiliary Air Force, Hendon, 1935.

600 Squadron adopted Red and White interlocking triangles in a band along the fuselage and across the top wing as its squadron markings. The 'weekend airmen', as the Auxiliary Air Force units were known, took the spotlight at the 1936 and 1937 Hendon Air Displays and were to thoroughly justify their skills and training in the forthcoming Battle of Britain. Fuselage roundels were 25 inches in diameter. Upper-wing roundels were 35 inches in diameter and under-wing roundels were 55 inches in diameter. Fuselage and rudder serials were 8 inches in height and in Black. Under-wing serials were also Black and were 30 inches in height.

Reference: p.9, *The Hart Family – Hawker Hart and Derivatives*, Aeroguide Classics No.5, Linewrights Ltd, 1989.

Not to any scale

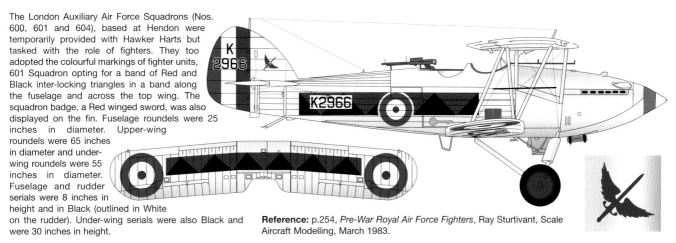

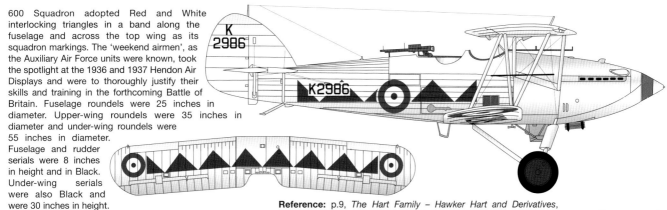

Hawker Demon, K4500, 604 (County of Middlesex) Squadron, Auxiliary Air Force, Hendon, 1936.

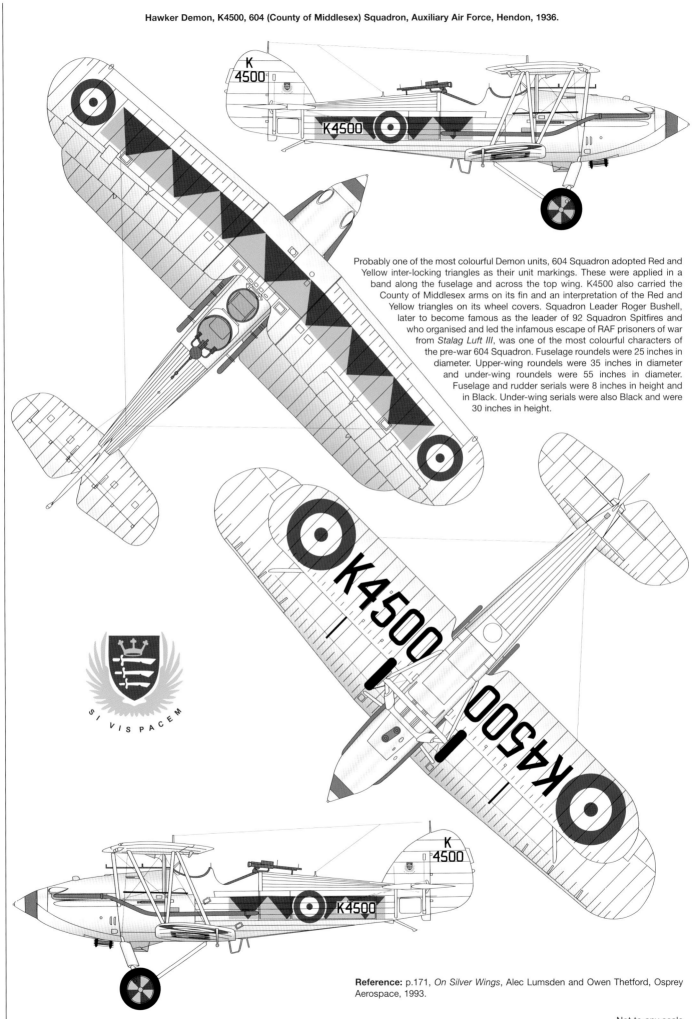

Probably one of the most colourful Demon units, 604 Squadron adopted Red and Yellow inter-locking triangles as their unit markings. These were applied in a band along the fuselage and across the top wing. K4500 also carried the County of Middlesex arms on its fin and an interpretation of the Red and Yellow triangles on its wheel covers. Squadron Leader Roger Bushell, later to become famous as the leader of 92 Squadron Spitfires and who organised and led the infamous escape of RAF prisoners of war from *Stalag Luft III*, was one of the most colourful characters of the pre-war 604 Squadron. Fuselage roundels were 25 inches in diameter. Upper-wing roundels were 35 inches in diameter and under-wing roundels were 55 inches in diameter. Fuselage and rudder serials were 8 inches in height and in Black. Under-wing serials were also Black and were 30 inches in height.

SI VIS PACEM

Reference: p.171, *On Silver Wings*, Alec Lumsden and Owen Thetford, Osprey Aerospace, 1993.

Not to any scale

Hawker Demon, K2905, 41 Squadron, Northolt, 1935.

Largely due to the threat to British interests posed by Mussolini's invasion of Abbysinia, the Demon saw much more overseas service than was customary of Home Defence fighter squadrons. 41 Squadron was shipped overseas in total, moving to first Aden then Egypt between October 1935 and August 1936. Fortunately, the squadron was not involved in the fighting and undertook no more than an 'air-policing' role. Fuselage roundels were 25 inches in diameter. Upper-wing roundels were 35 inches in diameter and under-wing roundels were 55 inches in diameter. Fuselage and rudder serials were 8 inches in height and in Black. Under-wing serials were also Black and were 30 inches in height.
Reference: p.177, *On Silver Wings*, Alec Lumsden and Owen Thetford, Osprey Aerospace, 1993.

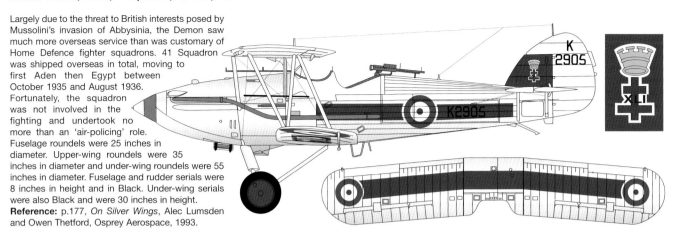

Hawker Demon, K4511, 208 Squadron, Heliopolis, Egypt, December 1935.

Although classed as an Army Co-operation Squadron, then flying Audaxes, 208 Squadron was increased with the introduction of a fourth flight of Demons. A new flight was formed as a result of Mussolini's invasion of Abbysinia and the need to protect British interests in the North African region. No squadron markings were used. Fuselage roundels were 25 inches in diameter. Upper-wing roundels were 35 inches in diameter and under-wing roundels were 55 inches in diameter. Fuselage and rudder serials were 8 inches in height and in Black. Under-wing serials were also Black and were 30 inches in height.
Reference: p.168, *On Silver Wings*, Alec Lumsden and Owen Thetford, Osprey Aerospace, 1993.

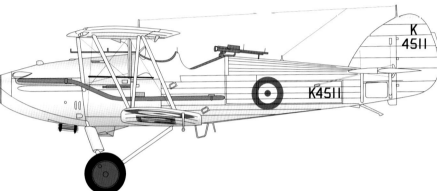

Hawker Demon, serial unknown, 74 Squadron, Hal Far, Malta 1935.

74 Squadron was formed en-route to Malta as part of the British Mediterranean defence force during the Abyssinian Crisis. During the crisis, the squadron's Demons were hastily camouflaged in this unusual scheme. The paints were locally produced with a mix of standard RAF colours and locally acquired paints. The serial numbers were usually painted over and the under surfaces and the metal struts were left in their original Aluminium doped finish. This Demon also retained its Red wheel discs and tail fin, indicating a machine of 'A' Flight. Note the single Red/Blue roundel, approximately 35 inches in diameter, on the top of the right upper-wing. The rear part of the exhaust was painted with a special White anti-glow paint, presumably to stop it from blinding the crew at night.

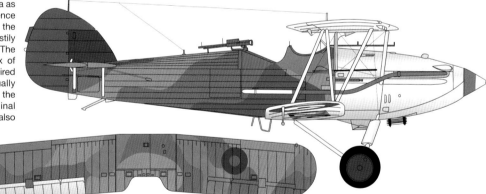

Reference: p.163, *Introducing RAF Camouflage*, Paul Lucas, Scale Aircraft Modelling, Volume 22, Number 3, May 2000.

Hawker Turret Demon, K5698, 23 Squadron, Biggin Hill, 1936.

Very few Turret Demons achieved the colourful markings of their predecessors. Most were limited to the fighter unit symbol of a White spearhead on the fin within which the squadron badge was positioned. Fuselage roundels were 25 inches in diameter. Upper-wing roundels were 35 inches in diameter and under-wing roundels were 55 inches in diameter. Fuselage and rudder serials were 8 inches in height and in Black. Under-wing serials were also Black and were 30 inches in height.
Reference: p.82, *Aircraft Camouflage and Markings 1907–1954*, Bruce Robertson, Harleyford Publications Limited, 1956.

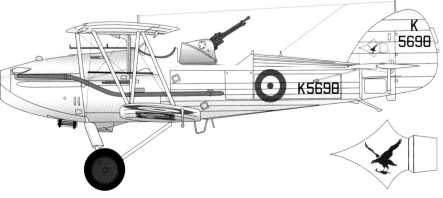

Not to any scale

Hawker Turret Demon, K5705, 23 Squadron, Biggin Hill, 1936.

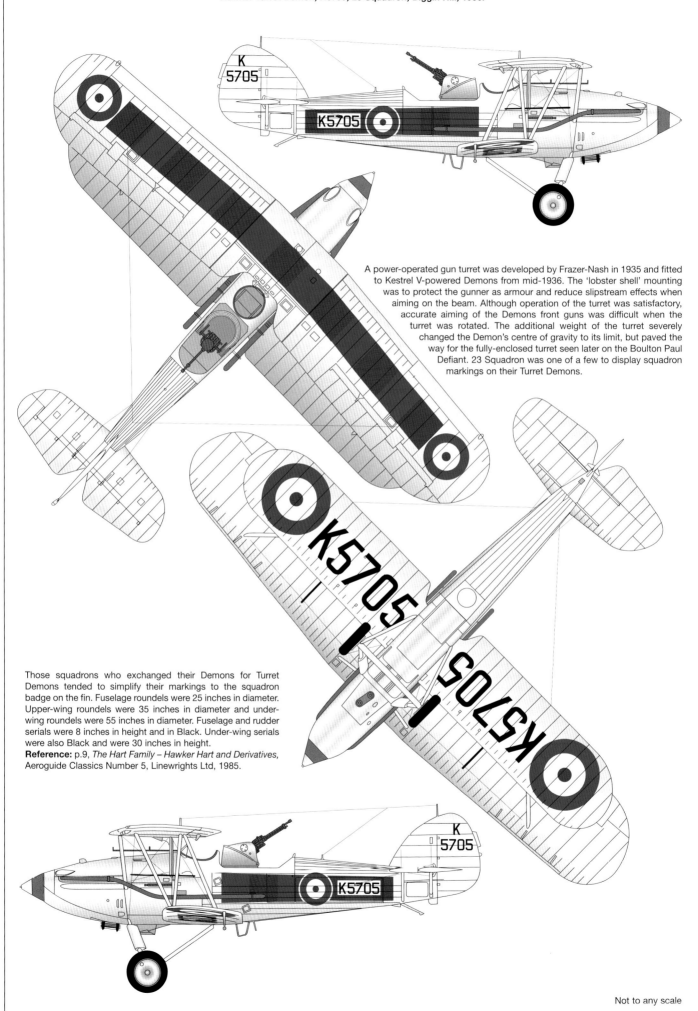

A power-operated gun turret was developed by Frazer-Nash in 1935 and fitted to Kestrel V-powered Demons from mid-1936. The 'lobster shell' mounting was to protect the gunner as armour and reduce slipstream effects when aiming on the beam. Although operation of the turret was satisfactory, accurate aiming of the Demons front guns was difficult when the turret was rotated. The additional weight of the turret severely changed the Demon's centre of gravity to its limit, but paved the way for the fully-enclosed turret seen later on the Boulton Paul Defiant. 23 Squadron was one of a few to display squadron markings on their Turret Demons.

Those squadrons who exchanged their Demons for Turret Demons tended to simplify their markings to the squadron badge on the fin. Fuselage roundels were 25 inches in diameter. Upper-wing roundels were 35 inches in diameter and under-wing roundels were 55 inches in diameter. Fuselage and rudder serials were 8 inches in height and in Black. Under-wing serials were also Black and were 30 inches in height.
Reference: p.9, *The Hart Family – Hawker Hart and Derivatives,* Aeroguide Classics Number 5, Linewrights Ltd, 1985.

Not to any scale

Hawker Fury I, K2048, 1 Squadron, Tangmere, April 1933. Squadron Commander's aircraft.

The squadron commander of 1 Squadron prominently displayed his pennant on the fin of his aircraft, providing a clear in-flight identification marking to his fellow pilots. The evolution of 1 Squadron's markings, can clearly be seen by comparing this aircraft with K5673 below. Fuselage roundels were 25 inches in diameter. Upper-wing roundels were 50 inches in diameter and under-wing roundels were 35 inches in diameter. Fuselage and rudder serials were 8 inches high and in Black (outlined in White on the rudder). The under-wing serials were 30 inches high and also painted Black.
Reference: p.138, *On Silver Wings*, Alec Lumsden and Owen Thetford, Osprey Aerospace, 1993.

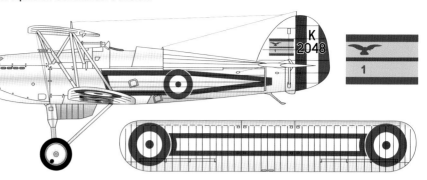

Hawker Fury I, K5673, 1 Squadron, Tangmere, 1935.

K5673 was a late production Fury I and shows the later style of 1 Squadron markings. Earlier aircraft displayed more open parallel Red bars and no fuselage serial. K5673 was also 'A' Flight leader's aircraft indicated by its Red fin and tail. Note also the squadron badge within the 'Spearhead' Fighter Unit symbol. This had become a standard marking for most fighter units by this period. Fuselage roundels were 25 inches in diameter. Upper-wing roundels were 40 inches in diameter and under-wing roundels were 35 inches in diameter. Fuselage and rudder serials were 8 inches high and in Black. The under-wing serials were 30 inches high and also painted Black.
Reference: p.144, *On Silver Wings*, Alec Lumsden and Owen Thetford, Osprey Aerospace, 1993.

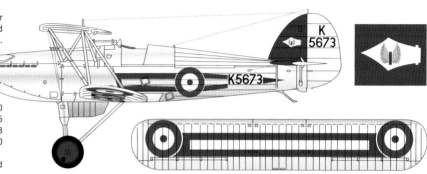

Hawker Fury II, K7279, 25 Squadron, Tangmere, 1935.

K7279 shows the standard squadron markings for 25 Squadron. The 'Spearhead' Fighter Unit symbol was integrated within a triangle which was painted in the aircraft's flight colour. Fuselage roundels were 25 inches in diameter. Upper-wing roundels were 40 inches in diameter and under-wing roundels were 35 inches in diameter. Fuselage and rudder serials were 8 inches high and in Black. The under-wing serials were 30 inches high and also painted Black.
Reference: p.500, *Born with a Sting – the Hawker Fury*, Richard J Caruana, Scale Aviation Modeller International, Volume 3, Issue 8, August 1997.

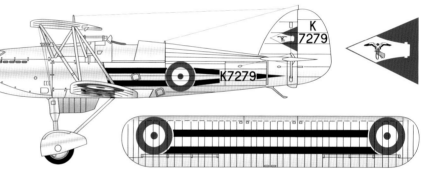

Hawker Fury I, K5682, Advanced Training Flight, RAF College Cranwell, 1936.

In addition to its fame as a front-line fighter aircraft, the Fury was equally respected by the eleven training establishments which were fortunate to acquire these machines. Some were passed on from the fighter squadrons, but many were late production batches direct from the factory. The Fury was able to provide the officer cadets with advanced training after they had passed their dual-control phase in Hawker Harts. Fuselage roundels were 25 inches in diameter. Upper-wing roundels were 40 inches in diameter and under-wing roundels were 35 inches in diameter. Fuselage and rudder serials were 8 inches high and in Black. The under-wing serials were 30 inches high and also painted Black.
Reference: p209, *The Hawker Fury*, Francis K. Mason, Aircraft in Profile Vol.1, 1-24, Profile Publications Ltd. 1965.

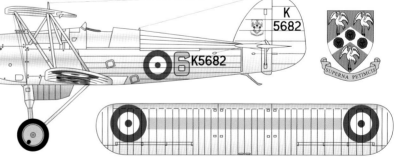

Hawker Fury I, K3736, 5 Flying Training School, Sealand, 1938.

K3736 displays the Trainer Yellow and polished metal finish that was distinctive of trainer aircraft in the late 1930s. Many future Battle of Britain pilots had their first experience of flying a fighter in the cockpit of a Fury. Fuselage roundels were 25 inches in diameter. Upper-wing roundels were 40 inches in diameter and under-wing roundels were 35 inches in diameter. Fuselage and rudder serials were 8 inches high and in Black. The under-wing serials were 30 inches high and also painted Black.
Reference: p.216, *The Hawker Fury*, Francis K. Mason, Aircraft in Profile Vol.1, 1–24, Profile Publications Ltd. 1965.

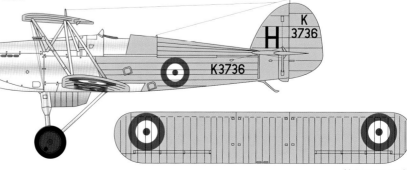

Not to any scale

Hawker Fury I, K2065, 1 Squadron, Tangmere, 1932.

1 Squadron received their Hawker Furys in 1932. K2065 was an early example with pre-1934 large roundels and rudder stripes. During this period, the squadron painted the top fuselage decking of their aircraft in flight colours. K2065 was the 'C' Flight leader's aircraft and so carried the additional markings of a Blue-coloured spinner, wheel covers and fin. Note the White disc behind the cockpit on the upper decking. This may be another flight leader identification symbol or space left free of paint for the arial connections. Also note the small identification letter on the port side engine panel. The squadron marking on early Furys was painted with the parallel Red bars widely spaced. On later aircraft, the bars were spaced closer together. Fuselage roundels were 25 inches in diameter. Upper-wing roundels were 50 inches in diameter and under-wing roundels were 35 inches in diameter. Rudder serials were 8 inches in height and painted Black, outlined in White. Under-wing serials were 30 inches in height and also in Black.

Reference: p.8, *Warpaint – Hawker Fury*, Aviation News.

Not to any scale

Hawker Fury I, K1930, 43 Squadron, Tangmere, June 1932. Squadron Leader W.E. Bryant, MBE.

43 Squadron was the first squadron to receive Furys in May 1931. A friendly rivalry developed between the Tangmere-based 43 and 1 Squadrons, both squadrons competed in the annual RAF Air Exercises and Hendon Air Displays. Squadron Leader Bryant's training of his aerobatics team included practice manoeuvres on the ground, with his pilots on bicycles! K1930 carried the Squadron Leader's markings of a Black chequered fin. Note that the fuselage and top wing chequers were Black on the natural metal finish of the aircraft, but with a Black outline around the edges. Fuselage roundels were 25 inches in diameter. Upper-wing roundels were 50 inches in diameter and under-wing roundels were 35 inches in diameter. Fuselage and rudder serials were 8 inches in height and in Black (rudder serials were outlined in White) and under-wing serials were 30 inches in height and also in Black.

Reference: p.152, *On Silver Wings*, Alec Lumsden and Owen Thetford, Osprey Aerospace, 1993.

Not to any scale

Hawker Fury II, K7270, 25 Squadron, Hawkinge, 1936. Squadron Leader A.L. 'Tony' Paxton.

25 Squadron was the third Fury squadron in the elite trio of aerobatic squadrons that delighted the Hendon Air Display crowds through the 1930s. Squadron Leader Paxton earned a footnote in RAF history when, in 1933, he led his formation team of nine aircraft in a tied together take-off. The squadron then broke into three flights and, still tied together, performed a series of individual aerobatics routines. 25 Squadron also achieved the fame of flying the fastest Fury in the RAF, setting the record at 223 mph. in a Fury II. Fuselage roundels were 25 inches in diameter. Upper-wing roundels were 40 inches in diameter and under-wing roundels were 35 inches in diameter. Fuselage and rudder serials were 8 inches in height and in Black, while the under-wing serials were 30 inches in height and also in Black.

References: p.12, *On Silver Wings, Part 16*, Owen Thetford, Aeroplane Monthly, January 1992.

Not to any scale

Hawker Fury II, K7266, 41 Squadron, Royal Air Force, Catterick, 1938.

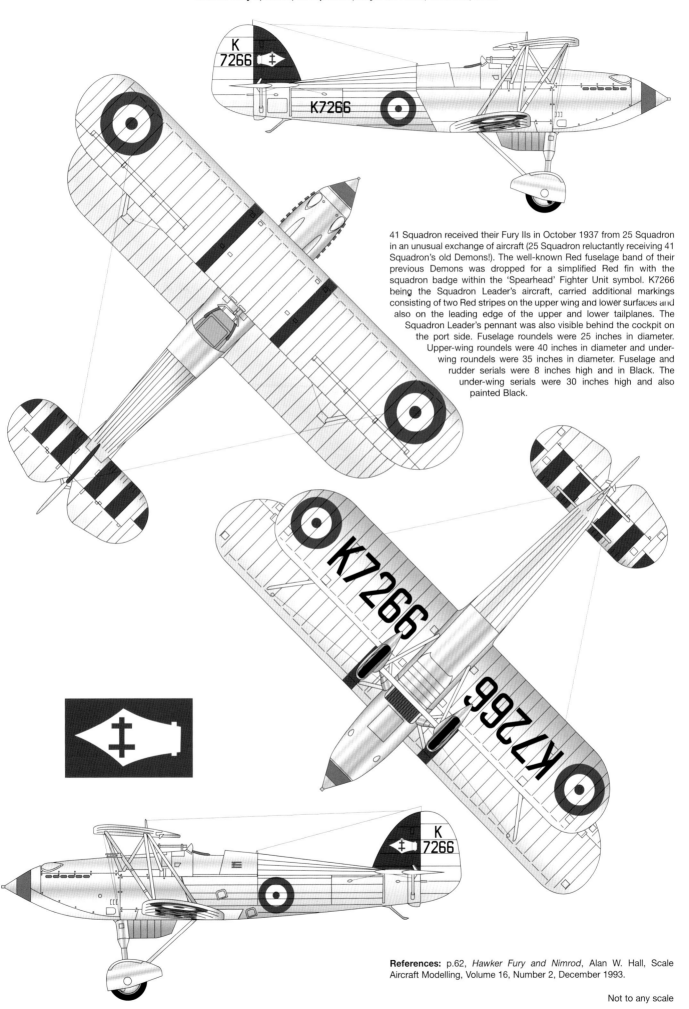

41 Squadron received their Fury IIs in October 1937 from 25 Squadron in an unusual exchange of aircraft (25 Squadron reluctantly receiving 41 Squadron's old Demons!). The well-known Red fuselage band of their previous Demons was dropped for a simplified Red fin with the squadron badge within the 'Spearhead' Fighter Unit symbol. K7266 being the Squadron Leader's aircraft, carried additional markings consisting of two Red stripes on the upper wing and lower surfaces and also on the leading edge of the upper and lower tailplanes. The Squadron Leader's pennant was also visible behind the cockpit on the port side. Fuselage roundels were 25 inches in diameter. Upper-wing roundels were 40 inches in diameter and under-wing roundels were 35 inches in diameter. Fuselage and rudder serials were 8 inches high and in Black. The under-wing serials were 30 inches high and also painted Black.

References: p.62, *Hawker Fury and Nimrod*, Alan W. Hall, *Scale Aircraft Modelling*, Volume 16, Number 2, December 1993.

Not to any scale

Gloster Gauntlet I, K4085, 19 Squadron, Northolt, June 1935.

19 Squadron was the first RAF unit to receive the Gauntlet I in May 1935. The aircraft soon became popular with pilots and public alike. In June 1935, the squadron won the Sir Phillip Sassoon Flight Attack Challenge Trophy and also spearheaded a 155-ship flypast for King George V's Jubilee Year at Duxford. In 1936, 19 Squadron Gauntlets thrilled the crowds at Hendon RAF Display with a polished three-ship 'tied together' display of aerobatics. Fuselage roundels were 25 inches in diameter. Upper- and lower-wing roundels were 35 inches in diameter. Fuselage and rudder serials were 8 inches high and in Black. Under-wing serials were 30 inches and also in Black.
Reference: p.187, *On Silver Wings*, Alec Lumsden and Owen Thetford, Osprey Aerospace 1993.

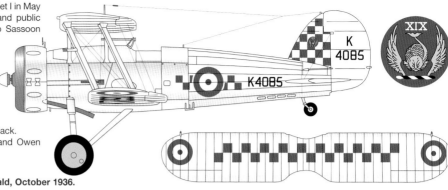

Gloster Gauntlet II, K5287, 56 Squadron, North Weald, October 1936.

56 Squadron's famous Red and White chequered markings continued during their spell with Gauntlets. However, an unusual layout on the fuselage stopped the marking quite short forward of the roundel. The squadron flew Gauntlets from May 1936 until July 1937 when they were re-equipped with Hawker Hurricanes. Fuselage roundels were 25 inches in diameter. Upper- and lower-wing roundels were 35 inches in diameter. Fuselage and rudder serials were 8 inches high and in Black. Under-wing serials were 30 inches and also in Black.
Reference: p.193, *On Silver Wings*, Alec Lumsden and Owen Thetford, Osprey Aerospace 1993.

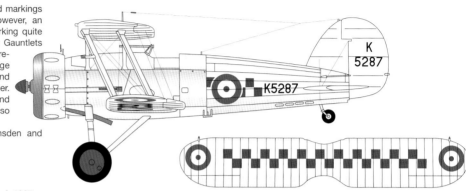

Gloster Gauntlet II, K7824, 66 Squadron, Duxford, 1937.

66 Squadron was reformed at Duxford from 'C' Flight of 19 Squadron on 20 July 1936. It took as its squadron markings, two pale Blue bars outlined in Black. These were parallel across the upper wing and tapered through the fuselage roundel. K7824 also carried the squadron emblem of a rattlesnake within the fighter unit spearhead on the fin. Fuselage roundels were 25 inches in diameter. Upper- and lower-wing roundels were 35 inches in diameter. Fuselage and rudder serials were 8 inches high and in Black. Under-wing serials were 30 inches and also in Black.
Reference: p.252, *Pre-war Royal Air Force Fighters*, Ray Sturtivant, Scale Aircraft Modelling, Volume 5, No.6, March 1983.

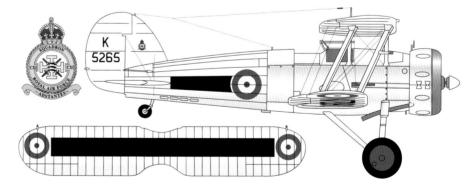

Gloster Gauntlet II, K5265., 111 Squadron, Northolt, 1938.

111 Squadron, together with 56 Squadron, were the first units to receive the Gauntlet II in 1936. They retained their famous Black bar marking, but this was severely abbreviated on the sides of the fuselage. K5265 also carried its new RAF badge on the fin – approved by King Edward VIII in October 1936. Fuselage roundels were 25 inches in diameter. Upper- and lower-wing roundels were 35 inches in diameter. Rudder serial was 8 inches high and in Black. Under-wing serials were 30 inches and also in Black.
Reference: p.252, *Pre-war Royal Air Force Fighters*, Ray Sturtivant, Scale Aircraft Modelling, Volume 5, No.6, March 1983.

Gloster Gauntlet II ,K5265, 111 Squadron, Northolt, 1938.

An unusual and mysterious development for K5265 above, is this reference of the aircraft without fuselage roundel and Black bar, but retaining the upper-wing bar. In place of the fuselage roundel, a large letter 'B' has been painted. There is no indication as to whether this marking was prior to, or after the view of K5265 in its standard scheme above. Upper- and lower-wing roundels were 35 inches in diameter. Rudder serial was 8 inches high and in Black. Under-wing serials were 30 inches and also in Black.
Reference: p.252, *Pre-war Royal Air Force Fighters*, Ray Sturtivant, Scale Aircraft Modelling, Volume 5, No.6, March 1983.

Not to any scale

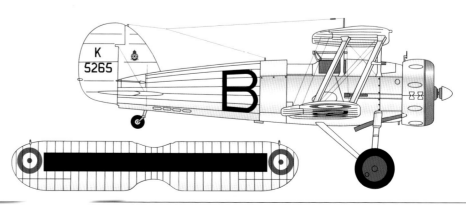

Gloster Gauntlet II, K5358, 17 Squadron, Kenley, 1937. Pilot: Squadron Leader H.Y. Humphreys.

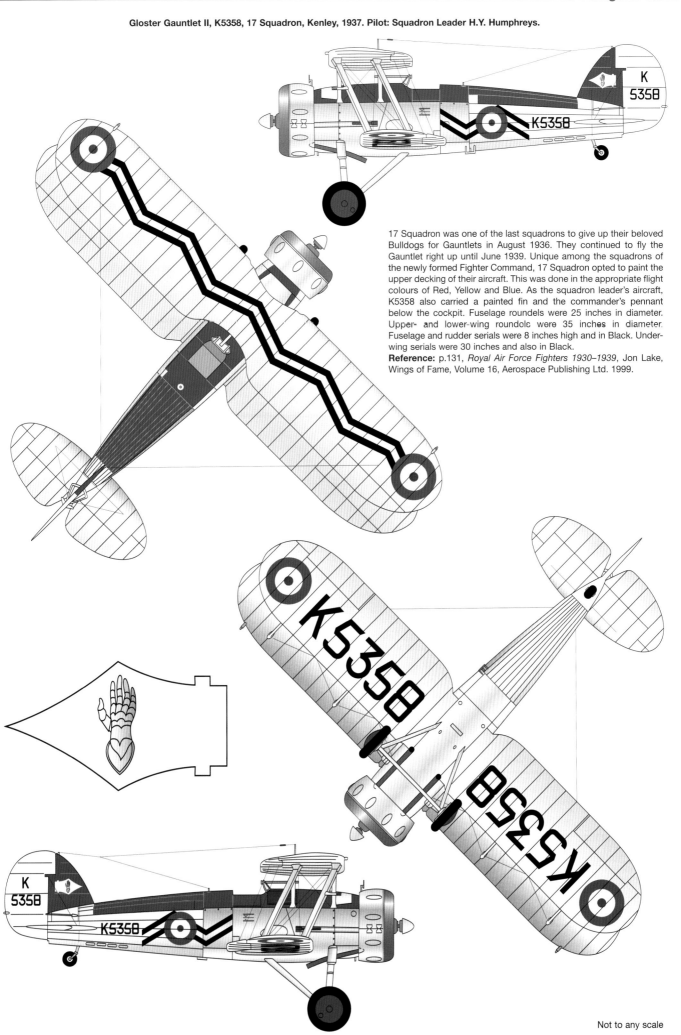

17 Squadron was one of the last squadrons to give up their beloved Bulldogs for Gauntlets in August 1936. They continued to fly the Gauntlet right up until June 1939. Unique among the squadrons of the newly formed Fighter Command, 17 Squadron opted to paint the upper decking of their aircraft. This was done in the appropriate flight colours of Red, Yellow and Blue. As the squadron leader's aircraft, K5358 also carried a painted fin and the commander's pennant below the cockpit. Fuselage roundels were 25 inches in diameter. Upper- and lower-wing roundels were 35 inches in diameter. Fuselage and rudder serials were 8 inches high and in Black. Under-wing serials were 30 inches and also in Black.

Reference: p.131, *Royal Air Force Fighters 1930–1939*, Jon Lake, Wings of Fame, Volume 16, Aerospace Publishing Ltd. 1999.

Not to any scale

Gloster Gauntlet II, K7796, 46 Squadron, Kenley, 1937.

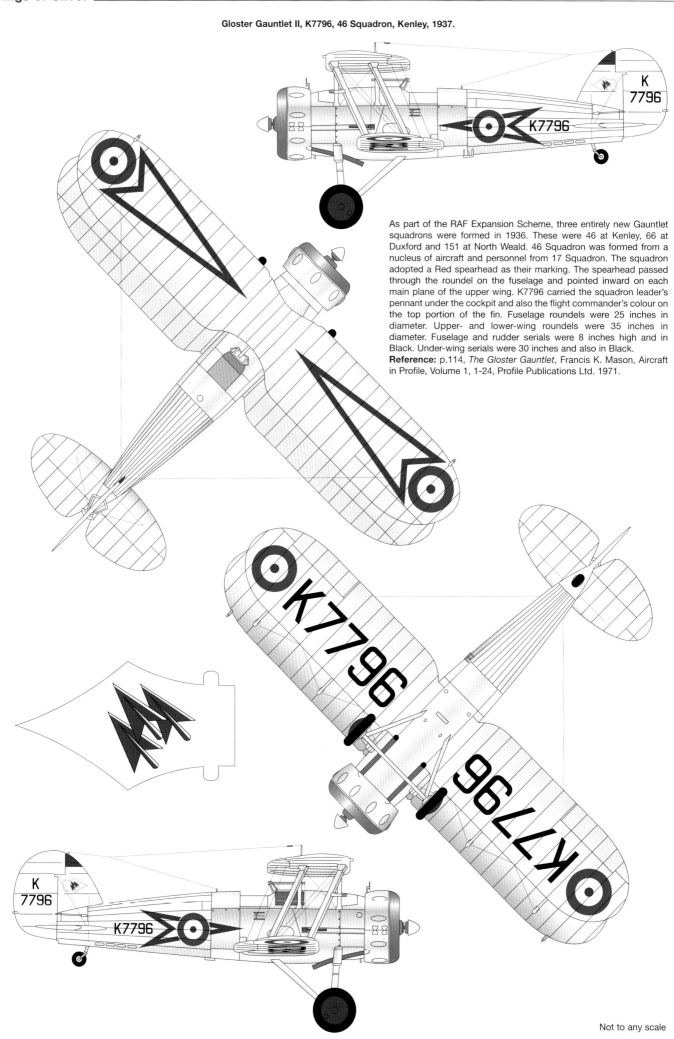

As part of the RAF Expansion Scheme, three entirely new Gauntlet squadrons were formed in 1936. These were 46 at Kenley, 66 at Duxford and 151 at North Weald. 46 Squadron was formed from a nucleus of aircraft and personnel from 17 Squadron. The squadron adopted a Red spearhead as their marking. The spearhead passed through the roundel on the fuselage and pointed inward on each main plane of the upper wing. K7796 carried the squadron leader's pennant under the cockpit and also the flight commander's colour on the top portion of the fin. Fuselage roundels were 25 inches in diameter. Upper- and lower-wing roundels were 35 inches in diameter. Fuselage and rudder serials were 8 inches high and in Black. Under-wing serials were 30 inches and also in Black.

Reference: p.114, *The Gloster Gauntlet*, Francis K. Mason, Aircraft in Profile, Volume 1, 1-24, Profile Publications Ltd. 1971.

Not to any scale

Gloster Gauntlet II, K7890, 151 Squadron, North Weald, 1937.

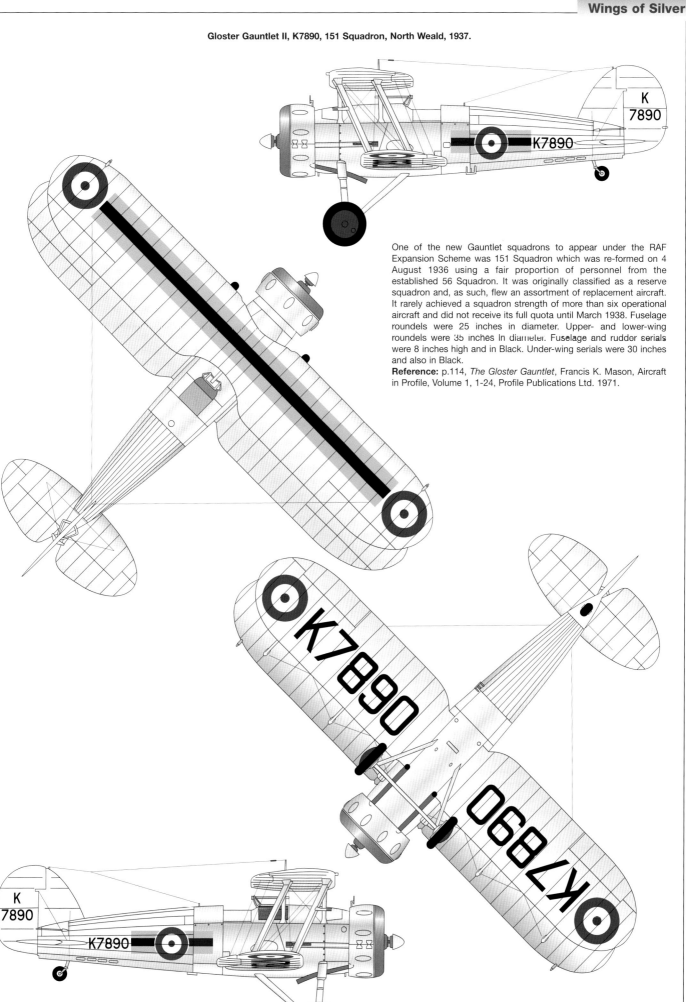

One of the new Gauntlet squadrons to appear under the RAF Expansion Scheme was 151 Squadron which was re-formed on 4 August 1936 using a fair proportion of personnel from the established 56 Squadron. It was originally classified as a reserve squadron and, as such, flew an assortment of replacement aircraft. It rarely achieved a squadron strength of more than six operational aircraft and did not receive its full quota until March 1938. Fuselage roundels were 25 inches in diameter. Upper- and lower-wing roundels were 35 inches in diameter. Fuselage and ruddor serials were 8 inches high and in Black. Under-wing serials were 30 inches and also in Black.

Reference: p.114, *The Gloster Gauntlet*, Francis K. Mason, Aircraft in Profile, Volume 1, 1-24, Profile Publications Ltd. 1971.

Not to any scale

Gloster Gauntlet II, K7810, 213 Squadron, Church Fenton, 1937.

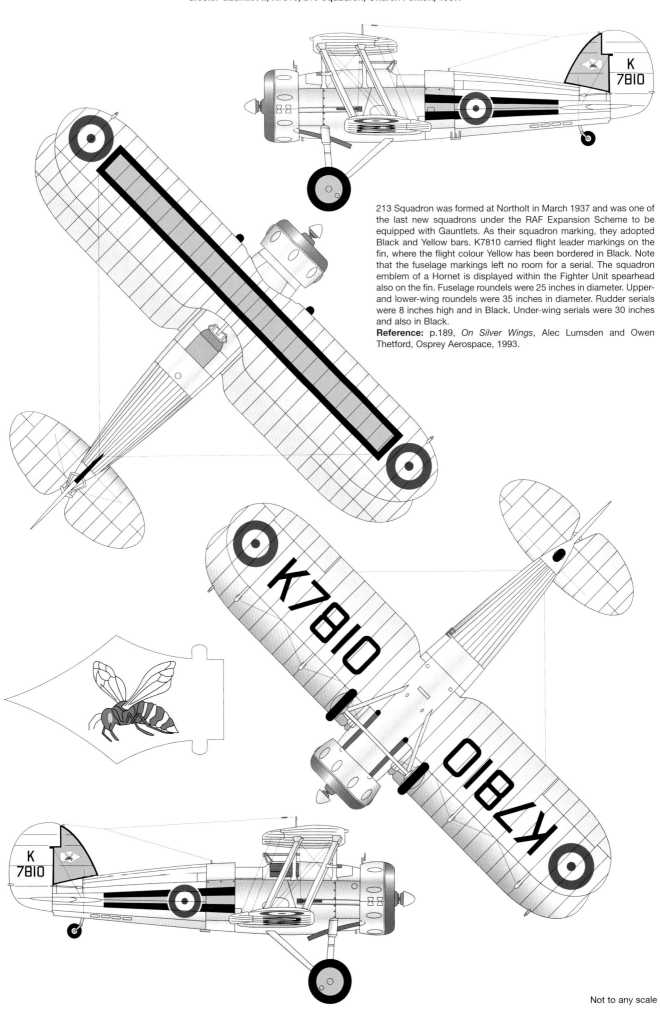

213 Squadron was formed at Northolt in March 1937 and was one of the last new squadrons under the RAF Expansion Scheme to be equipped with Gauntlets. As their squadron marking, they adopted Black and Yellow bars. K7810 carried flight leader markings on the fin, where the flight colour Yellow has been bordered in Black. Note that the fuselage markings left no room for a serial. The squadron emblem of a Hornet is displayed within the Fighter Unit spearhead also on the fin. Fuselage roundels were 25 inches in diameter. Upper- and lower-wing roundels were 35 inches in diameter. Rudder serials were 8 inches high and in Black. Under-wing serials were 30 inches and also in Black.

Reference: p.189, *On Silver Wings*, Alec Lumsden and Owen Thetford, Osprey Aerospace, 1993.

Not to any scale

Gloster Gauntlet II, K7862, 74 Squadron, Hornchurch, 1938.

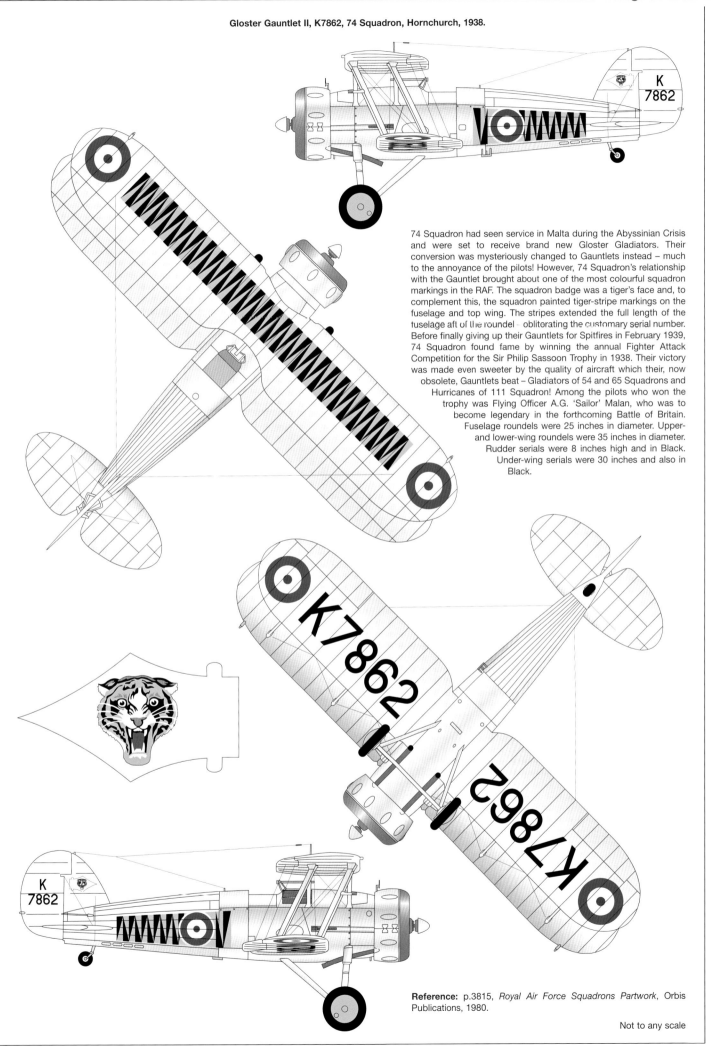

74 Squadron had seen service in Malta during the Abyssinian Crisis and were set to receive brand new Gloster Gladiators. Their conversion was mysteriously changed to Gauntlets instead – much to the annoyance of the pilots! However, 74 Squadron's relationship with the Gauntlet brought about one of the most colourful squadron markings in the RAF. The squadron badge was a tiger's face and, to complement this, the squadron painted tiger-stripe markings on the fuselage and top wing. The stripes extended the full length of the fuselage aft of the roundel – obliterating the customary serial number. Before finally giving up their Gauntlets for Spitfires in February 1939, 74 Squadron found fame by winning the annual Fighter Attack Competition for the Sir Philip Sassoon Trophy in 1938. Their victory was made even sweeter by the quality of aircraft which their, now obsolete, Gauntlets beat – Gladiators of 54 and 65 Squadrons and Hurricanes of 111 Squadron! Among the pilots who won the trophy was Flying Officer A.G. 'Sailor' Malan, who was to become legendary in the forthcoming Battle of Britain. Fuselage roundels were 25 inches in diameter. Upper- and lower-wing roundels were 35 inches in diameter. Rudder serials were 8 inches high and in Black. Under-wing serials were 30 inches and also in Black.

Reference: p.3815, *Royal Air Force Squadrons Partwork*, Orbis Publications, 1980.

Not to any scale

Gloster Gladiator I ,K7943, 65 Squadron, Hornchurch, 1937.

65 Squadron's markings remain a mystery as no reference can be found to show that the previous Gauntlet fuselage and wing marking, of Red chevrons were continued on their Gladiators. The squadron commander's aircraft, K7943, displayed the chevron marking in a low key way on its fin. However, as many RAF squadrons were replacing their fuselage and wing markings with fin badges during this period, 65 Squadron may well have decided to follow this trend. Fuselage roundels were 25 inches in diameter. Upper-wing and lower-wing roundels were 40 inches in diameter. Fuselage and rudder serials were Black and 8 inches in height. Under-wing serials were also Black and 20 inches in height.

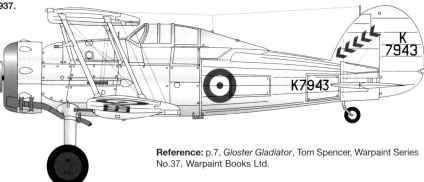

Reference: p.7, *Gloster Gladiator*, Tom Spencer, Warpaint Series No.37, Warpaint Books Ltd.

Gloster Gladiator I, L7620, SO-O, 33 Squadron, Ramleh, Palestine 1938.

33 Squadron was deployed Egypt in 1935 to protect the Suez Canal. By 1938, detachments were sent to Palestine keeping the peace between Arab and Jewish factions. L7620 displayed the pre-war squadron code letters SO-O in Light Grey. However, reference shows that other aircraft in the flight were still without codes at this time. Fuselage roundels were 25 inches in diameter. Upper-wing and lower-wing roundels were 40 inches in diameter. Fuselage and rudder serials were Black and 8 inches in height. Under-wing serials were also Black and 20 inches in height.
Reference: p.15 *Gloster Gladiator* by Tom Spencer, Warpaint Series No.37, Warpaint Books Ltd.

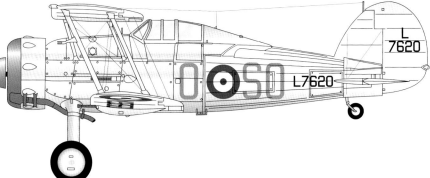

Gloster Gladiator I, K7903, 80 Squadron, Ismalia, Egypt, 1938.

80 Squadron was dispatched to Egypt in 1938 to protect British interests in the Middle East. They were to remain in Egypt and Libya until November 1940. No squadron markings were used apart from the squadron badge appearing inside the spearhead symbol on the fin. K7903 was the 'A' Flight commander's aircraft, denoted by the Red fin. Fuselage roundels were 25 inches in diameter. Upper-wing and lower-wing roundels were 40 inches in diameter. Fuselage and rudder serials were Black and 8 inches in height. Under-wing serials were also Black and 20 inches in height.
Reference: p.13, *Gloster Gladiator*, Tom Spencer, Warpaint Series No.37, Warpaint Books Ltd.

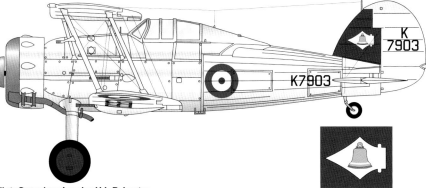

Gloster Gladiator I, K7960, 3 Squadron, Kenley, 1938. Pilot: Squadron Leader H.L.P. Lester.

By 1938, 3 Squadron had removed its Green squadron markings from the fuselage and upper wing of their aircraft. Following the move to more simplified squadron identification, they opted to show the squadron number on the fin in the appropriate flight colour. Squadron Leader Lester identified his aircraft by placing the number on a Black and Green sunburst background. Note also the introduction of individual, aircraft identification code letter 'P' on the fuselage. This was painted in Light Grey and was approx. 30 inches in height. Fuselage roundels were 25 inches in diameter. Upper-wing and lower-wing roundels were 40 inches in diameter. Fuselage and rudder serials were Black and 8 inches in height. Under-wing serials were also Black and 20 inches in height.

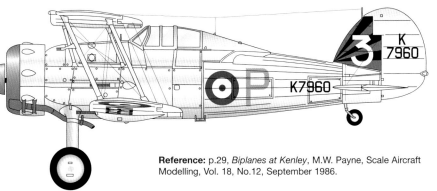

Reference: p.29, *Biplanes at Kenley*, M.W. Payne, Scale Aircraft Modelling, Vol. 18, No.12, September 1986.

Gloster Gladiator I, K7960, 3 Squadron, Kenley, August 1938. Pilot: Squadron Leader H.L.P. Lester.

Another view of K7960 at a slightly later date. The aircraft is seen in the process of being camouflaged. It appears that only the metal parts had been painted at this point in time, upper- and lower-wing surfaces also remaining in their aluminium doped finish. Note the remains of the old fin marking and over-painting of serials. Fuselage roundels were 25 inches in diameter. Upper-wing and lower-wing roundels were 40 inches in diameter. Fuselage and rudder serials were Black and 8 inches in height. Under-wing serials were also Black and 20 inches in height.
Reference: *Biplanes at Kenley*, M. W. Payne, Scale Aircraft Modelling, Vol. 18, No.12, September 1986.

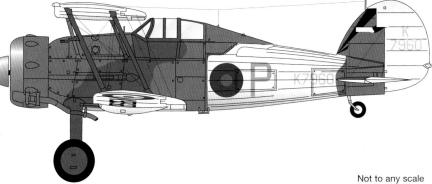

Not to any scale

Gloster Gladiator I, K6147, 3 Squadron, Kenley 1937.

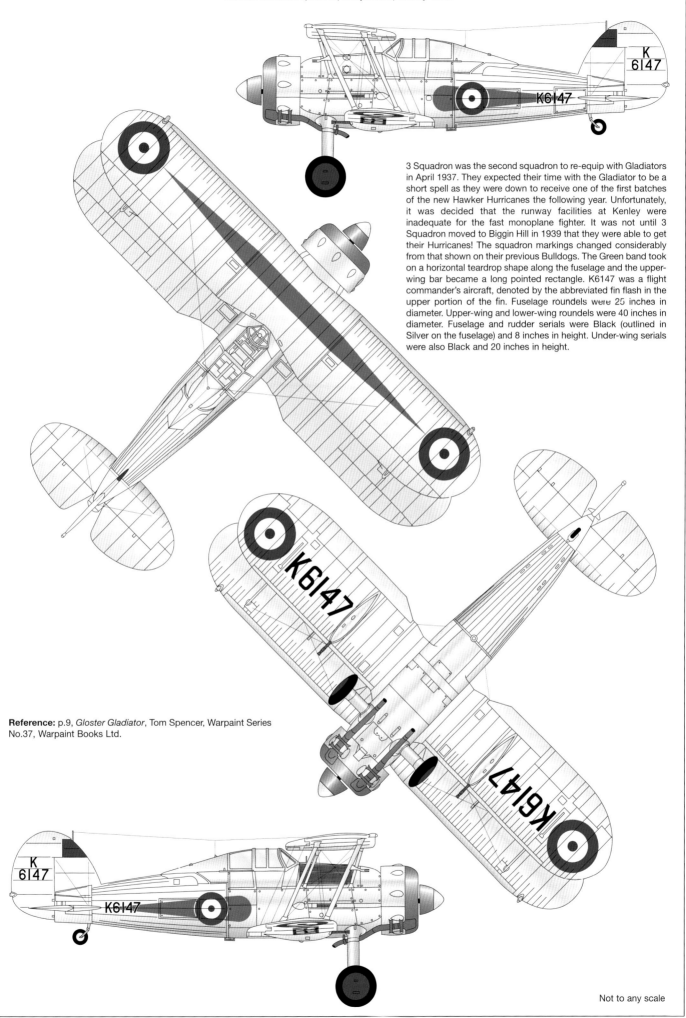

3 Squadron was the second squadron to re-equip with Gladiators in April 1937. They expected their time with the Gladiator to be a short spell as they were down to receive one of the first batches of the new Hawker Hurricanes the following year. Unfortunately, it was decided that the runway facilities at Kenley were inadequate for the fast monoplane fighter. It was not until 3 Squadron moved to Biggin Hill in 1939 that they were able to get their Hurricanes! The squadron markings changed considerably from that shown on their previous Bulldogs. The Green band took on a horizontal teardrop shape along the fuselage and the upper-wing bar became a long pointed rectangle. K6147 was a flight commander's aircraft, denoted by the abbreviated fin flash in the upper portion of the fin. Fuselage roundels were 25 inches in diameter. Upper-wing and lower-wing roundels were 40 inches in diameter. Fuselage and rudder serials were Black (outlined in Silver on the fuselage) and 8 inches in height. Under-wing serials were also Black and 20 inches in height.

Reference: p.9, *Gloster Gladiator*, Tom Spencer, Warpaint Series No.37, Warpaint Books Ltd.

Not to any scale

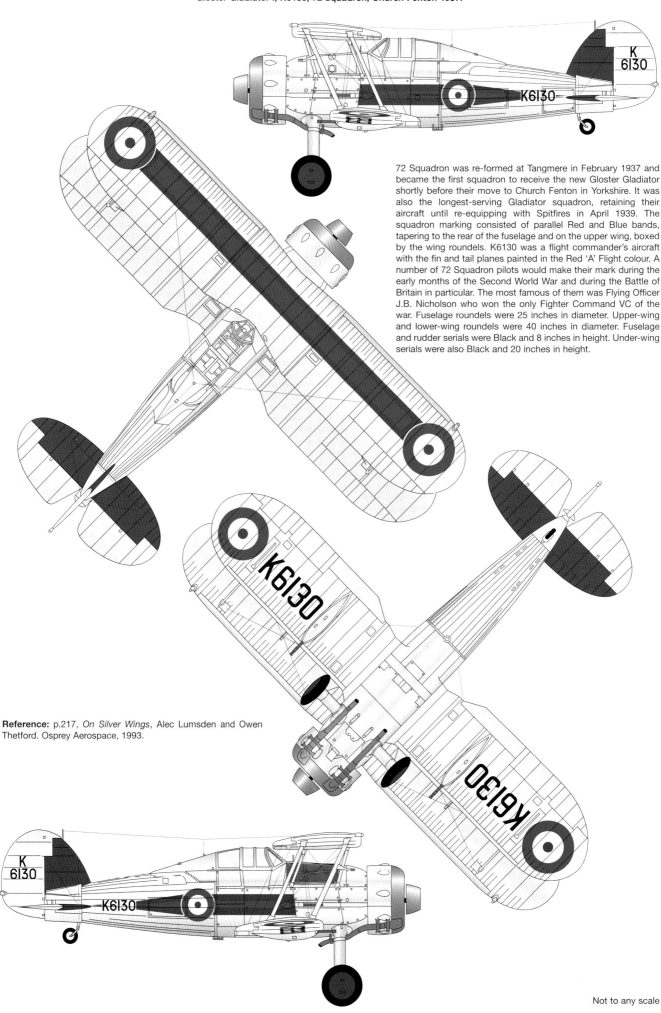

Gloster Gladiator I, K6130, 72 Squadron, Church Fenton 1937.

72 Squadron was re-formed at Tangmere in February 1937 and became the first squadron to receive the new Gloster Gladiator shortly before their move to Church Fenton in Yorkshire. It was also the longest-serving Gladiator squadron, retaining their aircraft until re-equipping with Spitfires in April 1939. The squadron marking consisted of parallel Red and Blue bands, tapering to the rear of the fuselage and on the upper wing, boxed by the wing roundels. K6130 was a flight commander's aircraft with the fin and tail planes painted in the Red 'A' Flight colour. A number of 72 Squadron pilots would make their mark during the early months of the Second World War and during the Battle of Britain in particular. The most famous of them was Flying Officer J.B. Nicholson who won the only Fighter Command VC of the war. Fuselage roundels were 25 inches in diameter. Upper-wing and lower-wing roundels were 40 inches in diameter. Fuselage and rudder serials were Black and 8 inches in height. Under-wing serials were also Black and 20 inches in height.

Reference: p.217, *On Silver Wings*, Alec Lumsden and Owen Thetford. Osprey Aerospace, 1993.

Not to any scale

Gloster Gladiator I, K7985, 73 Squadron, Digby 1937. Pilot: Flying Officer E.J. 'Cobber' Kain.

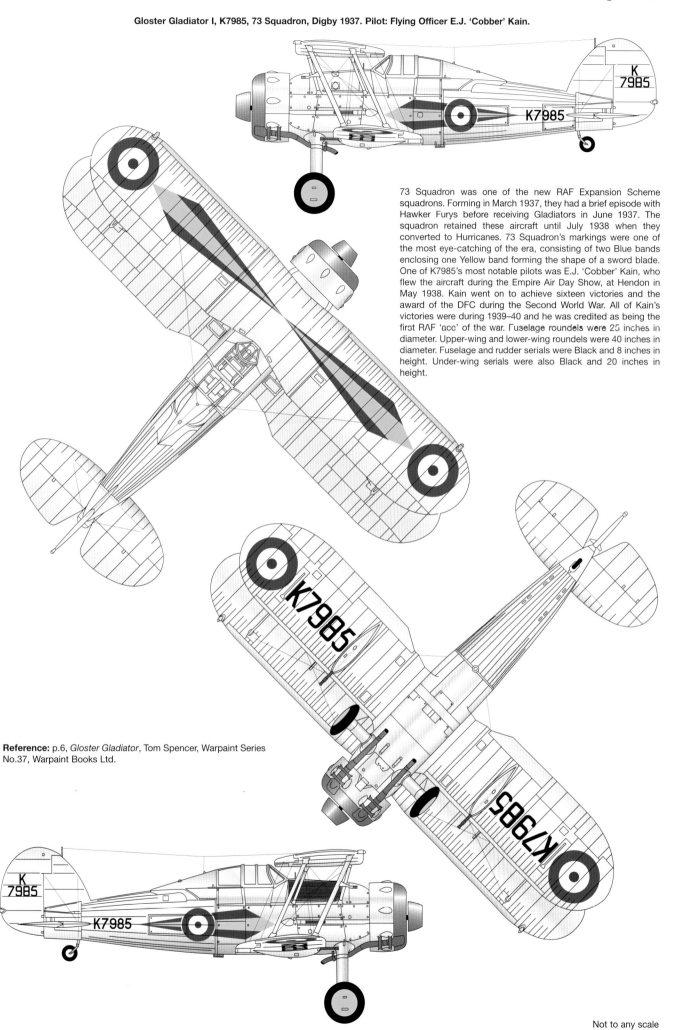

73 Squadron was one of the new RAF Expansion Scheme squadrons. Forming in March 1937, they had a brief episode with Hawker Furys before receiving Gladiators in June 1937. The squadron retained these aircraft until July 1938 when they converted to Hurricanes. 73 Squadron's markings were one of the most eye-catching of the era, consisting of two Blue bands enclosing one Yellow band forming the shape of a sword blade. One of K7985's most notable pilots was E.J. 'Cobber' Kain, who flew the aircraft during the Empire Air Day Show, at Hendon in May 1938. Kain went on to achieve sixteen victories and the award of the DFC during the Second World War. All of Kain's victories were during 1939–40 and he was credited as being the first RAF 'ace' of the war. Fuselage roundels were 25 inches in diameter. Upper-wing and lower-wing roundels were 40 inches in diameter. Fuselage and rudder serials were Black and 8 inches in height. Under-wing serials were also Black and 20 inches in height.

Reference: p.6, *Gloster Gladiator*, Tom Spencer, Warpaint Series No.37, Warpaint Books Ltd.

Not to any scale

Gloster Gladiator I, K7956, 3 Squadron, Kenley, August 1938.

K7956 carried the later abbreviated 3 Squadron marking on the fin and it is assumed that this was painted in the flight colour. 3 Squadron were also, at this time, beginning to use individual aircraft identification codes in the form of letters approximately 30 inches high and in Grey. While participating in air exercises at Sutton Bridge, K7956 undershot the runway and overturned while landing. Fuselage roundels were 25 inches in diameter. Upper-wing and lower-wing roundels were 40 inches in diameter. Fuselage and rudder serials were Black and 8 inches in height. Under-wing serials were also Black and 20 inches in height.
Reference: p.27, *Gloster Gladiator*, Philip Jarrett, Aeroplane Magazine, August 2000.

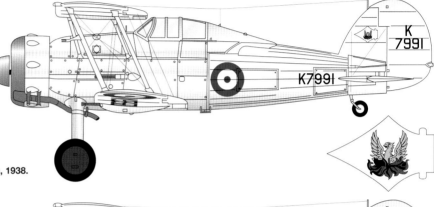

Gloster Gladiator I, K7991, 56 Squadron, North Weald, 1938.

56 Squadron chose to discontinue using their famous Red and White chequer board markings while flying Gladiators. Subsequently, their only marking was the squadron phoenix badge within the spearhead symbol on the aircraft's fin. Their time with Gladiators was quite short, flying the type for only ten months before converting to Hurricanes in May 1938. Fuselage roundels were 25 inches in diameter. Upper-wing and lower-wing roundels were 40 inches in diameter. Fuselage and rudder serials were Black and 8 inches in height. Under-wing serials were also Black and 20 inches in height.
Reference: p.11 *Gloster Gladiator* by Tom Spencer, Warpaint Series No.37, Warpaint Books Ltd.

Gloster Gladiator I, K8004, 72 Squadron, Church Fenton, 1938.

Towards the latter part of their service with Gladiators, 72 Squadron discarded their earlier Red and Blue squadron markings and decorated their aircraft solely with the squadron badge inside the spearhead symbol on the fin. Noticeable even before the Munich Crisis of September 1938, Gladiator squadrons were marking their aircraft in more modest ways than previously shown on other types. Fuselage roundels were 25 inches in diameter. Upper-wing and lower-wing roundels were 40 inches in diameter. Fuselage and rudder serials were Black and 8 inches in height. Under-wing serials were also Black and 20 inches in height.

Reference: p.219, *On Silver Wings*, Alec Lumsden and Owen Thetford, Osprey Aerospace, 1993.

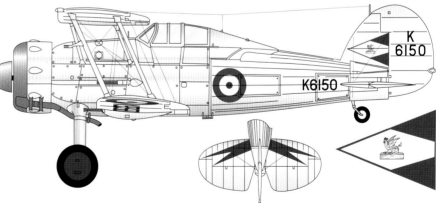

Gloster Gladiator I, K6150, 3 Squadron, Kenley, January 1938.
Pilot: Flight Sergeant E.H. Lomas.

When first issued with the Gladiator in March 1937, 3 Squadron's markings consisted of the squadron badge within a triangle on the fin. It is assumed that the triangle was in the appropriate flight colour and the White portion represented an abstracted spearhead shape. Strangely, K6150 clearly showed tail markings as illustrated in the scrap view, but no evidence is available that shows whether this marking was also applied to the upper wings. Unfortunately, Flight Sergeant Lomas had to abandon K6150 in a spin and it crashed into a front garden in Lyndhurst Road, Hove, Sussex. Fuselage roundels were 25 inches in diameter. Upper-wing and lower-wing roundels were 40 inches in diameter. Fuselage and rudder serials were Black and 8 inches in height. Under-wing serials were also Black and 20 inches in height.
Reference: p.213, *On Silver Wings*, Alec Lumsden and Owen Thetford, Osprey Aerospace, 1993.

Gloster Gladiator I, L7612, 33 Squadron, Ismailia, Egypt, March 1938.

Until 33 Squadron arrived in Egypt in March 1938, there had been no single-seat fighter squadrons stationed outside the UK since 1 Squadron left Iraq in 1926. Squadron markings consisted of the squadron badge, its famous Hart's head, within the customary spearhead symbol on the fin. Fuselage roundels were 25 inches in diameter. Upper-wing and lower-wing roundels were 40 inches in diameter. Fuselage and rudder serials were Black and 8 inches in height. Under-wing serials were also Black and 20 inches in height.
Reference: p.134, *Royal Air Force Fighters 1930–1939*, Jon Lake, Wings of Fame, Vol. 16, Aerospace Publishing Ltd. 1999.

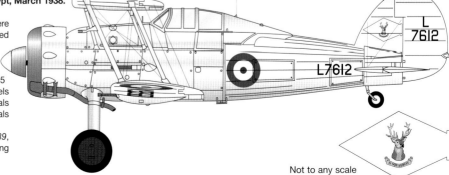

Not to any scale

Gloster Gladiator I, K8027, 87 Squadron, Debden 1938. Pilot: Flying Officer G.H.J. Feeny.

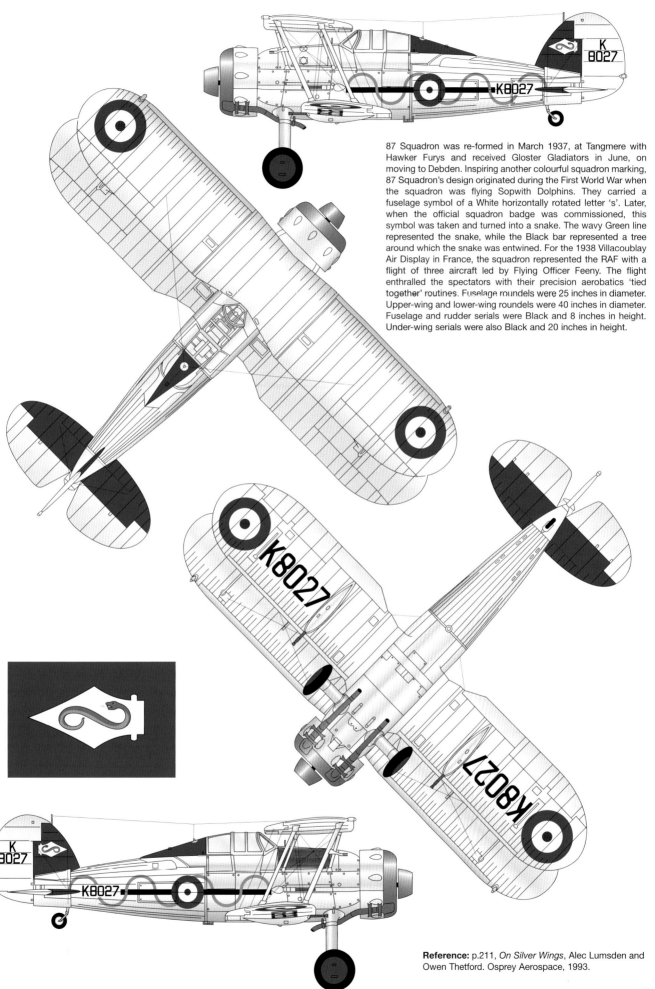

87 Squadron was re-formed in March 1937, at Tangmere with Hawker Furys and received Gloster Gladiators in June, on moving to Debden. Inspiring another colourful squadron marking, 87 Squadron's design originated during the First World War when the squadron was flying Sopwith Dolphins. They carried a fuselage symbol of a White horizontally rotated letter 's'. Later, when the official squadron badge was commissioned, this symbol was taken and turned into a snake. The wavy Green line represented the snake, while the Black bar represented a tree around which the snake was entwined. For the 1938 Villacoublay Air Display in France, the squadron represented the RAF with a flight of three aircraft led by Flying Officer Feeny. The flight enthralled the spectators with their precision aerobatics 'tied together' routines. Fuselage roundels were 25 inches in diameter. Upper-wing and lower-wing roundels were 40 inches in diameter. Fuselage and rudder serials were Black and 8 inches in height. Under-wing serials were also Black and 20 inches in height.

Reference: p.211, *On Silver Wings*, Alec Lumsden and Owen Thetford. Osprey Aerospace, 1993.

Not to any scale

Hawker Hind, K5457, AO-M, 211 Squadron, El Daba, Egypt, October 1938.

211 Squadron was re-formed as a day bomber unit at Mildenhall in June 1937. Re-equipped with the Hawker Hind, the squadron was posted to RAF Middle East Command, Egypt, in April 1938, shortly before the Munich Crisis. As with most other overseas units, the squadron's aircraft remained in their Silver finish. However, squadron codes were applied to the fuselage. The squadron's main base was at Helwan, but a detachment was sent to El Daba during September-October 1938. Fuselage roundels were 25 inches in diameter. Upper-wing roundels were 35 inches in diameter and under-wing roundels were 55 inches in diameter. Rudder serials were in Black and 8 inches in height while under-wing serials were 30 inches in height. Squadron codes were approximately 30 inches in height and in Medium Sea Grey.

Reference: *No.211 Squadron RAF*, www.211squadron.org by D.R. Clark and others, 1998–2006.

Hawker Turret Demon, K5698, MS-G, 23 Squadron, Tangmere, Wittering, 1938.

Individual squadrons responded differently to the order to camouflage their aircraft. While most squadrons kept rigidly to the camouflage colours of Dark Green/Dark Earth/Light Green/Light Earth and Night/White, other details were at the squadron's discretion. K5698, for example, retained its bright Red/White/bright roundels and wing control surfaces were left Silver. Also, to avoid the confusion of anonymity, the last two digits of the serial were chalked on to the rudder! At the time of the Munich Crisis, there were three regular RAF squadrons and five Auxiliary Air Force squadrons still operating the Hawker Demon. Fuselage roundels were 25 inches in diameter. Upper-wing roundels were 35 inches in diameter and under-wing roundels were 55 inches in diameter. Squadron codes were approximately 30 inches in height and in Medium Sea Grey.

Reference: p.83, *Aircraft Camouflage and Markings 1907–1954*, Bruce Robertson, Harleyford Publications Limited, 1956.

Hawker Fury, 43 Squadron, Tangmere, October 1938.

43 Squadron removed all evidence of squadron identity apart from retaining their squadron badge within the fin spearhead symbol. Upper-wing roundels were removed and under-wing roundels painted over in Night. The fuselage roundels were 25 inches in height but repainted in Red and Blue. Although squadron codes (NQ) were allocated, there is no evidence that 43 Squadron ever applied them during this period. Only 1, 41 and 43 Squadrons, plus some of the Flying Training Schools, were flying Furys at the time of the Munich Crisis.
Reference: p.16 *On Silver Wings* by Owen Thetford, Part 16, Aeroplane Monthly, January 1992.

Gloster Gauntlet II, K7854, RR-K, 615 (County of Surrey) Squadron, Kenley, December 1938.

In total, there were twelve Gauntlet squadrons in service at the time of the Munich Crisis. Most of them adopted the new squadron codes along with their Dark Green/Dark Earth/Light Green/Light Earth and Night/White camouflage. 79 Squadron, which specialised in night fighter duties had their Gauntlets painted all Black during this period. The fuselage roundel was the original 25 inches in diameter Red/White Blue roundel re-painted in the dull Red/Blue scheme. Wing roundels may have been similarly adapted, or alternatively painted Black, and were 35 inches in diameter. Squadron codes were approximately 30 inches in height and painted in Medium Sea Grey.
Reference: p.340, *Pre-war RAF Codes*, Andrew Thomas, Aviation News, 22 August–4 September 1986.

Gloster Gladiator, I FZ-O, 65 Squadron, Hornchurch, 1938.

Larger than normal squadron codes were applied to 65 Squadron's Gladiators and a smaller roundel was re-painted on the fuselage. Note the ailerons and under surfaces of the tail planes have retained their Silver finish. There were six UK-based Gladiator squadrons at the time of the Munich Crisis. A further two were based in Egypt and retained their Silver finish up until the outbreak of war. The fuselage roundel was repainted in the dull Red/Blue scheme but at the same time was reduced in to approximately 20 inches in diameter. Squadron codes were approximately 36 inches in height and painted in Medium Sea Grey.
Reference: p.16, *Gloster Gladiator*, Tom Spencer, Warpaint Series No.37, Warpaint Books Ltd.

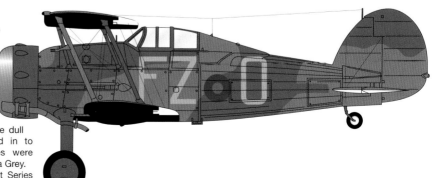

Not to any scale

F.36/34 Single-Seater Fighter, High-Speed Monoplane Hawker Hurricane prototype, K5083, Brooklands, 1935.
Pilot: Flight Lieutenant P.W.S. 'George' Bulman.

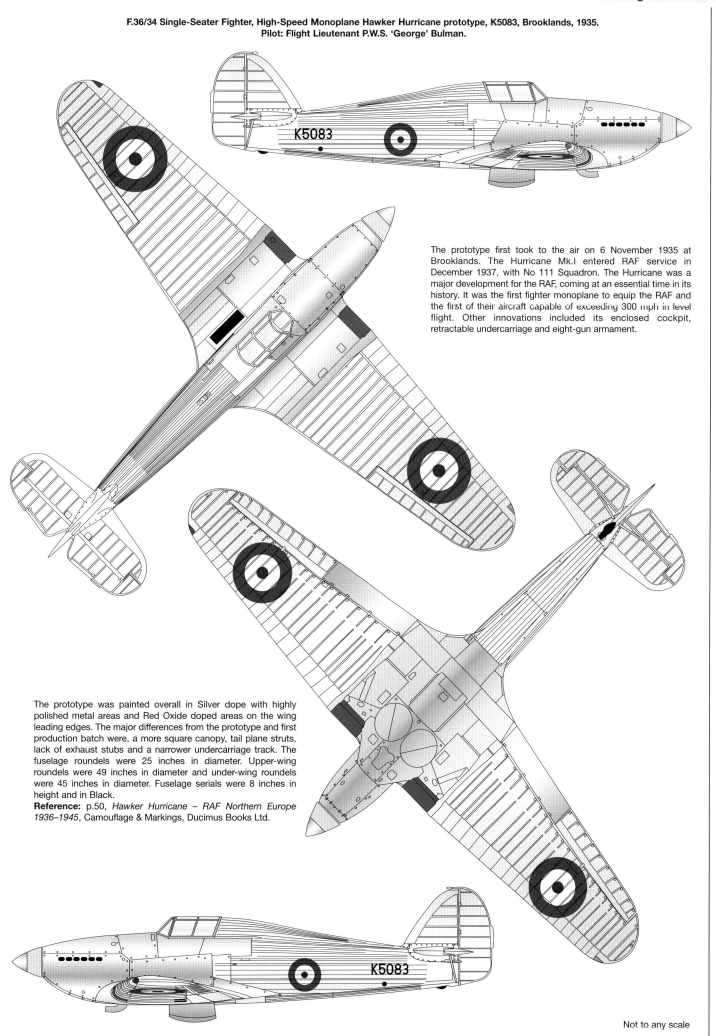

The prototype first took to the air on 6 November 1935 at Brooklands. The Hurricane Mk.I entered RAF service in December 1937, with No 111 Squadron. The Hurricane was a major development for the RAF, coming at an essential time in its history. It was the first fighter monoplane to equip the RAF and the first of their aircraft capable of exceeding 300 mph in level flight. Other innovations included its enclosed cockpit, retractable undercarriage and eight-gun armament.

The prototype was painted overall in Silver dope with highly polished metal areas and Red Oxide doped areas on the wing leading edges. The major differences from the prototype and first production batch were, a more square canopy, tail plane struts, lack of exhaust stubs and a narrower undercarriage track. The fuselage roundels were 25 inches in diameter. Upper-wing roundels were 49 inches in diameter and under-wing roundels were 45 inches in diameter. Fuselage serials were 8 inches in height and in Black.
Reference: p.50, *Hawker Hurricane – RAF Northern Europe 1936–1945*, Camouflage & Markings, Ducimus Books Ltd.

Not to any scale

Supermarine Type 300, K5054, Spitfire prototype, Eastleigh Airport, 6 March 1936. Pilot: 'Mutt' Summers, Supermarine chief test pilot.

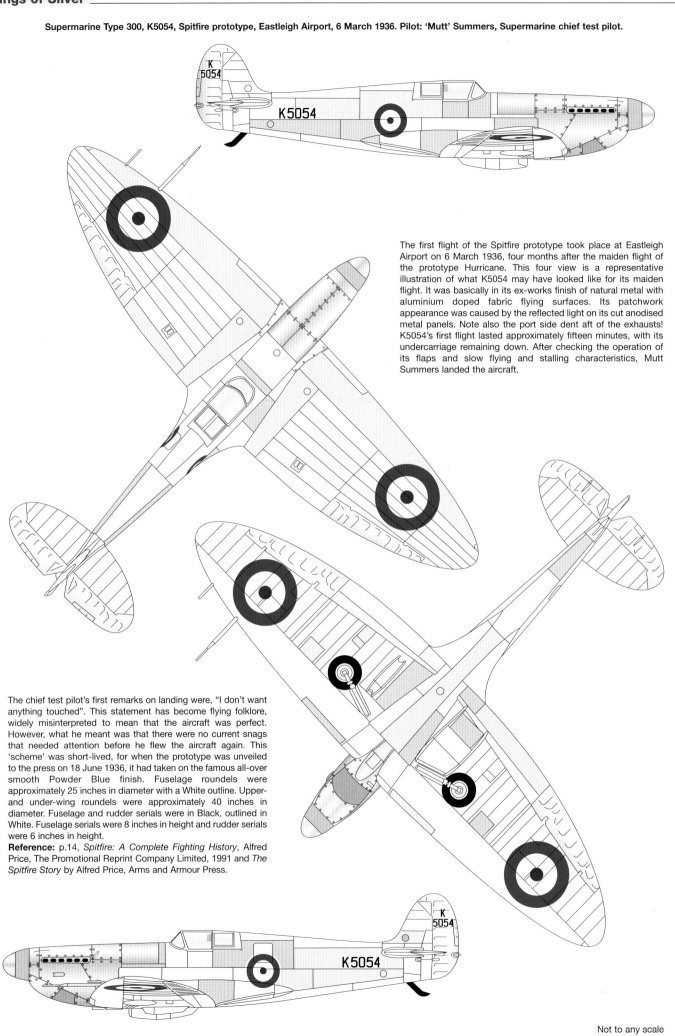

The first flight of the Spitfire prototype took place at Eastleigh Airport on 6 March 1936, four months after the maiden flight of the prototype Hurricane. This four view is a representative illustration of what K5054 may have looked like for its maiden flight. It was basically in its ex-works finish of natural metal with aluminium doped fabric flying surfaces. Its patchwork appearance was caused by the reflected light on its cut anodised metal panels. Note also the port side dent aft of the exhausts! K5054's first flight lasted approximately fifteen minutes, with its undercarriage remaining down. After checking the operation of its flaps and slow flying and stalling characteristics, Mutt Summers landed the aircraft.

The chief test pilot's first remarks on landing were, "I don't want anything touched". This statement has become flying folklore, widely misinterpreted to mean that the aircraft was perfect. However, what he meant was that there were no current snags that needed attention before he flew the aircraft again. This 'scheme' was short-lived, for when the prototype was unveiled to the press on 18 June 1936, it had taken on the famous all-over smooth Powder Blue finish. Fuselage roundels were approximately 25 inches in diameter with a White outline. Upper- and under-wing roundels were approximately 40 inches in diameter. Fuselage and rudder serials were in Black, outlined in White. Fuselage serials were 8 inches in height and rudder serials were 6 inches in height.

Reference: p.14, *Spitfire: A Complete Fighting History*, Alfred Price, The Promotional Reprint Company Limited, 1991 and *The Spitfire Story* by Alfred Price, Arms and Armour Press.

Not to any scale